CUCINA del
VENETO

CUCINA del
VENETO

DELICIOUS RECIPES FROM
VENICE & NORTHEAST ITALY

Ursula Ferrigno

photography by **Clare Winfield**

RYLAND PETERS & SMALL
LONDON • NEW YORK

Dedication

To Antonia, for your interest in the Veneto from the tender age of five when we visited, for licking your lips and always smiling and wanting 'fish with eyes please Mummy'!

Senior Designer Toni Kay
Senior Editor Abi Waters
Head of Production
  Patricia Harrington
Creative Director
  Leslie Harrington
Editorial Director Julia Charles

Wine Expert Richard Lagani
Food Stylist Kathy Kordalis
Prop Stylist Zoe Harrington
Indexer Vanessa Bird

First published in 2024 by
Ryland Peters & Small
20-21 Jockey's Fields, London
WC1R 4BW
and
341 E 11th St
New York, NY 10029

10 9 8 7 6 5 4 3 2 1

Illustration credits:
Front jacket artwork: Vibrands Studio
Spine: smash338

Printed in China.

ISBN: 978-1-78879-607-1

A CIP record for this book is available
from the British Library.
US Library of Congress cataloging-in-
Publication Data has been applied for.

NOTES

• All spoon measurements are level unless otherwise specified.
• All eggs are medium (UK) or large (US), unless specified as large, in which case US extra-large should be used. Uncooked or partially cooked eggs should not be served to the very old, frail, young children, pregnant women or those with compromised immune systems.
• When a recipe calls for cling film/ plastic wrap, you can substitute for beeswax wraps, silicone stretch lids or compostable baking paper for greater sustainability.
• When a recipe calls for the grated zest of citrus fruit, buy unwaxed fruit and wash well before using.
• Ovens should be preheated to the specified temperatures. If using a fan-assisted oven, adjust temperatures according to the manufacturer's instructions.

FSC
MIX
Paper from responsible sources
FSC® C106563
www.fsc.org

CONTENTS

Venice and the Veneto have been part of my life since childhood. I was eleven the first time I visited Venice. I know the province of Verona well, where the radicchio my father exported was grown. Food connected me to the Veneto as a child, and it still does now, as I teach at a cookery school in the Dolomite foothills of Treviso three times a year. To be able to visit so often, and to cook with the region's magical ingredients, is a privilege and pleasure.

A BRIEF HISTORY OF THE VENETO

This is not a history book, but I think knowing something about the region's social and political history is important to understanding many facets of its culinary history. Veneto was part of the Roman Empire until the 5th century AD, after which parts of the north were invaded by Germanic barbarians. Seeking safety, many local people moved south to the Adriatic coast. Here they found marshes, lagoons and islands, all of which formed a natural barrier to invasion, and several island communities were established. These formed the basis of today's Venice and its numerous islands.

Venice gradually became a powerful and rich city because of its geographical location, straddling trade routes from East to West, with access to the Mediterranean. The Republic of Venice – traditionally known as *La Serenissima* ('the most serene') – was established in 697 AD. During the Middle Ages it ruled most of northern Italy, as well as lands on the eastern side of the Adriatic (the modern Croatia, etc.) until 1797. During those 1,100 years, Venice's Republic was probably the largest, richest trade empire in the world, with a monopoly in salt, pepper, sugar, coffee and spices such as cinnamon and saffron.

And because of the trading wealth of the Republic, the arts flourished in Veneto, with many famous painters, musicians, sculptors and architects living and working there. The beauty of Venice is testament to their talent and creativity.

Modern Veneto is divided into seven provinces, which are named after their provincial capitals: Belluno, Padova (Padua), Rovigo, Treviso, Vicenza, Verona and Venezia (Venice).

THE TERRAFERMA

The cooking of the seven provinces of Veneto is as diverse as the many landscapes of the region, from the snowy peaks of the Pre-Alps to the coastal marshes and lagoons.

North and inland from Venice and the sea, the dishes of the *terraferma* (mainland) are usually substantial. Meat is eaten instead of seafood, and the cooking is heartier, with many meat stews. The accompaniments to these, throughout the whole of Veneto, are polenta and rice, not pasta. Surprisingly, *baccalà* – dried cod in Veneto – is popular (cod is not found in the Mediterranean, and has to be imported).

In mountainous Belluno, wild mushrooms abound in season. In Treviso, with its fertile soil, radicchio is king, and it is also where I teach, in the wonderful village of Cison de Valmarino. In Vicenza, the white asparagus from Bassano is a seasonal treat. (The Vicenzans were once called *mangiagatti*, 'cat eaters', due to some sad story concerning rats, cats and poverty, but I assure you the Vicenzan menu is completely cat-free now...) Padua is famous for its white polenta, preserved goose and wonderful chickens, while Verona is known for its gnocchi, fresh-water fish from Lake Garda, horsemeat stew, and vialone nano rice. (This is IGP, *Indicazione Geografica Protetta*, meaning that a food has unique qualities, and has been developed in a specific geographical area). Rovigo sits on the Adriatic, like Venice, and loves its fish and wild birds.

Most of the provinces make cheeses, salami and hams (Veneto ham is DOP, *Denominazione d'Origine Protetta*, 'protected designation of origin'). Veneto is a well-known wine area, producing many famous reds, wonderful Prosecco, and is also the home of grappa, the Italian equivalent of French marc.

VENICE

Venice, *La Serenissima*, is arguably the most beautiful and charismatic city of Italy. Its history as a maritime republic and its trade with the East have both helped to shape its culinary arsenal. In many of the seafood and other dishes, there are little touches of the exotic - the highly peppered sauce that accompanies duck and game dishes, a hint of cinnamon in risotto or gnocchi - which are rare in the rest of Italy. In Venice you should eat seafood, which is brought in fresh every day from the lagoon. Try sardines in an Arabic-influenced sweet and sour marinade; or *moleche* (soft-shelled crabs), or *bigoli in salsa*, pasta with an anchovy sauce. There are a few meat and poultry dishes worth trying, such as calf's liver with onions, *fegato alla veneziana*, duck with that characteristic pepper sauce, or the famous *carpaccio* invented in Harry's Bar. And do not miss the *cicchetti*, the snacks which you can try at any time of day, preferably with a glass of Prosecco.

I love the cooking of Venice, I love the city, I love its sense of theatre, its beauty - I often feel that I'm living in a glorious painting! I love its culture - from Carnevale, to the Biennale and Film Festival, to its wonderful concerts, theatres, museums and art galleries. I also bemoan its vulnerability for, despite safeguards in the lagoon, the sea still intrudes, and the *acqua alta* (high water) constantly threatens the ancient city's foundations.

I have been teaching cookery in Veneto for 20 years. I worked in Venice itself for four years, a two-week course every year. I got to know the city well, although every time I visit now, I seem to take a completely different path to the centre! I too was taught: I learned about risotto from Venetian chefs. They said a wooden spoon with a hole in it was the best implement, and that you should stir towards your heart. (My engineer husband assured me that there was no scientific reasoning behind either of these ideas. Science sometimes is a little boring...)

I also learned more about fish. I have been going to the same man in the Rialto fish market for 14 years now. He knows what I want, doesn't pressure me, and understands that sometimes I don't need the fish gutted, skinned or scaled (we will do that in class). I spend a lot of money so he is willing to accede to my sometimes curious requests. (He always manages to slip a packet of *baccalà* into my cool bag, even though I have told him we don't much like it!) Now, when I come into Venice from Treviso on market day (Tuesday), I can nod and smile at the vendors, as I have become a familiar face to them. They treat me like they would a Venetian, not a tourist, and indeed I quite often *feel* like a Venetian!

My feelings for Venice go even deeper, though. After returning from honeymoon (in 2003), I was teaching in Venice, my first time away from my new husband. One day, not feeling all that well, I somehow found my way to Caffè Florian in St Mark's Square: I couldn't eat anything, but I had such a longing for a cup of their hot chocolate. I didn't know it then, but I was already pregnant with my daughter, Antonia.

Every visit to Venice makes me feel as if I am discovering something new and special. For instance, I recently found a bookshop, the Libreria Acqua Alta, that has been flooded so many times it keeps its books in baths and boats, even a gondola! Venice, for me, has inspiration on every corner.

WINES OF THE VENETO

BY RICHARD LAGANI

Located in the northeast corner of Italy, the region of Veneto runs from Lake Garda in the west to the region's capital, Venice, and from the foothills of the Italian Alps in the north to the plains of the Po River in the South. With such diversity, the region contains some of the most beautiful landscapes in Italy. Veneto's geography, culture and wines represent the different peoples who have inhabited the region over the centuries. The region has historically been a crossroads for armies and merchants and can be seen as a transition between the Austrian and German influences of the Alps, and more Roman lands to the south.

Given this diversity, it comes as no surprise the region also produces some of the most beautiful wines in the world. What might be surprising is the Veneto region, although smaller than more well-known wine producing regions, produces more wine than Piedmont, Tuscany, Lombardy or Puglia. At one point, the region suffered from concerns of overproduction and quality, but today over one quarter of the region's wines are designated either Denominazione di Origine Contrallata 'DOC' or Denominazione di Origine Contrallata e Garantta 'DOCG', the two highest quality levels in Italian wine.

For those familiar with the French wine term Appellation d'Origine Controllée or 'AOC' these two Italian terms are similar and help consumers gauge the quality of the wine inside. DOC on a bottle means the wine adheres to the requirements and rules of the area where it was made. DOCG, the highest level of wine in Italy, requires the wine to pass a taste test as well as meet all the areas' requirements. Classico is another useful Italian wine term. A wine is only permitted to say Classico if it has been produced in the 'classic' or traditional area within the region where the wine was originally made. Depending on the area, Classico may also mean the winery has adhered to even more stringent wine-making requirements. While by no means foolproof, DOC or DOCG and Classico on the label generally indicate a higher quality wine.

While the rest of the world recognizes wines like Soave, Prosecco, Valpolicella and Amarone, often the people of Veneto drink wines made from other local indigenous grapes. As is the case with the rest of Europe, over 90% of the wines produced in Italy, stay in Italy. In addition, there is a beauty in the day-to-day simplicity of life in Veneto. Wines created from lesser-known varieties like Tai Rosso,

Dindarella and Verdiso are never far from the region's dining tables. There is even a French influence, a relic from Napoleon's occupation of the region, in that Merlot, Chardonnay, Cabernet Sauvignon and Sauvignon Blanc are grown alongside more traditional Italian grapes.

In terms of importance, the two most significant grape varieties in Veneto are Garganega and Corvina. The first is used in producing Soave and the second in the production of Valpolicella and Amarone.

Soave is made using the Garganega grape. While blending with other white grapes such as Trebbiano di Soave or Chardonnay is permitted, to qualify as a DOC or DOCG, the wine must contain a minimum of 70% Garganega. Soave is a versatile wine that not only pairs well with food and lifts a meal, but is also wonderful to drink on its own. It is a fresh, dry wine with floral aromas and high acid, which delightfully balances the apple, peach and citrus fruit flavours. The very best Soaves carry DOC/DOCG and Classico on their labels. This is vital as the original area is far better at producing wine than some of the other flatter, lower areas.

Valpolicella and Amarone are produced using the Corvina grape and are often blended with Rondinella and Molinara. Generally, Valpolicella and (its cousin Bardolino) are made in the normal way, creating soft, velvety dry wines with red fruit flavours and a slightly bitter almond finish. Amarone, on the other hand, is made using the same grape but only after they have been air-dried for several months and then fermented in the late winter. These dried, almost raisiny, grapes produce a wine that is dry but powerful, with intense flavours of ripe red fruits, raisins and baking spices.

These grapes also produce amazingly balanced sweet wines, Recioto di Soave and Recioto della Valpolicella. Like Amarone, these wines are made from partially dried grapes but are fermented to a luscious sweetness of stewed fruit flavours balanced with high acidity. The Recioto di Soave has a sweet, full-bodied flavour of candied citrus peels with a crisp finish. Recioto della Valpolicella is full of red fruit flavours with raisins, honey and a very clean finish. There is also an indulgent, slightly sparkling version that is amazing with any chocolate dessert.

No matter where you are in Veneto, you will find lovely wines to enjoy on their own or together with the regional cuisine. Whether you opt for an easy drinking Soave or a bold Amarone, or even a local lesser-known variety such as Tai Rosso, the wines of Veneto should not be missed.

SMALL BITES

CICCHETTI

DELIGHTFUL LITTLE MORSELS

I think it is impossible to visit Venice only once; you have to return again and again to properly absorb every enticing nuance. And for foodies, what is probably most enticing are the colourful shopfronts which, throughout the city, offer a varied array of snacks, the famous and unique Venetian *cicchetti*. These shopfronts usually belong to a *bacaro*, or wine bar, although you can also find *cicchetti* sold in a *ciccheteria, cantina, botega, enoteca* or *osteria*.

The word *cicchetti* – pronounced 'chiketti' – is said to derive from the Latin word, *ciccus*, which means 'little' or 'nothing'. *Cicchetti* are the Italian version of the Spanish *tapas*, tasty morsels to be eaten with a drink. As with *tapas*, you can make a meal of *cicchetti*, by ordering multiple plates, for a good and filling meal. And you don't necessarily have to eat and drink in the same *bacaro* – you could make your way from *bacaro* to *bacaro*, sampling the varied tastes on offer, as well as differing wines. It is a good way of familiarizing yourself with the labyrinthine side-streets of the city.

A glass of wine is the usual accompaniment to a *cicchetto*. This glass is called *ombra*, meaning 'shade' or 'shadow', said to be a reminder of the days when wines were unloaded from boats on to the Riva degli Schiavoni, the broad avenue along the

waterfront from St Mark's Square (now probably the most popular promenade in the world). The wines were sold from shaded stalls which, throughout the day, had to move as the sun moved. The words 'wine' and 'shade' became so inextricably linked that *'Andemo bever un'ombra'* ('let's go to drink a shadow') is now simply the Venetian way of inviting you to go for a drink. The wines in *bacari* are normally local, from the Veneto, which are very reasonable in price, and are usually served from the tap, rather than from bottles. Occasionally, nowadays, an *ombra* refers to an Aperol spritz, the luminous orange drink that has become so popular in the last ten years or so.

Bacari are normally situated in the *calli* (the maze of alleys) off the main Venetian thoroughfares, and are easily identifiable because, in good (or

indeed indifferent) weather, there will be a huddle of people standing outside with small glasses in their hands. Inside are shelves of assorted *cicchetti*, beautifully arranged, colourful and irresistible. The Venetians eat *cicchetti* in the morning, towards lunch, or in the afternoon as a snack. I must admit that, in the tiny *cicchetti* bar next to the Rialto cheese shop, I have often seen locals enjoying their Prosecco and *cicchetti* at ten in the morning!

You don't have to speak Italian to order, you can just point. You normally eat standing up, using your fingers or a cocktail stick. In a small city where space is at a premium, eating on the hoof, so to speak, makes more sense than sitting down in a restaurant, which takes more time and is much more expensive. (Although I urge you to eat in as many of Venice's restaurants as you can; many are superb.) With *cicchetti*, you can eat as much or as little as you like, and you can enjoy a selection of flavours and textures, which is much more interesting than simply an appetizer and main.

Cicchetti are designed to stimulate the appetite, so they are quite big on flavour (which is not mild, it is often sweet and sour, *agrodolce*). The foods on offer vary from tiny sandwiches to pâtés, olives, salami, eggs, cooked meats and fish, mostly served on small slices of bread or set polenta. In the summer, the *cicchetti* are smaller and lighter, perhaps using vegetable and salad ingredients. In winter, there might be heavier fare, such as a stew, served on or in a roll. Many *cicchetti* served with a sauce are offered on small plates. *Baccalà mantecato* and *sarde in saor* are two famous Venetian dishes, which are shrunk to *cicchetti* size, but you can also encounter meatballs, baby octopus, sardines, crab and shrimp, squid, roasted vegetables and cheese combinations. *Nervetti* – veal and pork cartilage – are boiled and dressed and served as a *cicchetti*. This might not be to the taste of most non-Italians....

For me, one of the most enthralling aspects of Venetian *cicchetti* is that the menus in *bacari* change not only seasonally, but day by day, often – how can they do it? – hour by hour!

ROASTED PEPPER & TUNA CICCHETTI

PEPERONI ARROSTITI CON TONNO

I love the variety of textures, colours and flavours in this simple cicchetti, designed to bring the taste buds to anticipatory life.

1 yellow (bell) pepper

1 red (bell) pepper

6 plum tomatoes

½ ciabatta loaf, cut into thin slices and toasted

8 tablespoons extra virgin olive oil

400 g/14 oz. can tuna in spring water, drained and flaked

2 tablespoons chopped fresh parsley

2 tablespoons chopped fresh basil

2 tablespoons rinsed and chopped capers

12 black olives, stoned/pitted

2 tablespoons red wine vinegar

sea salt and freshly ground black pepper

Serves 4–6

Preheat the oven to 200°C/180°C fan/400°F/Gas 6. Put the red and yellow peppers on a baking sheet and roast in the hot oven for 20 minutes. Leave until cool enough to handle, then peel away the skins. Halve, core and deseed the peppers, then cut into strips, saving the juices.

Immerse the tomatoes in boiling water for 10 seconds, then drain and peel away the skins. Quarter, core and deseed the tomatoes, then roughly chop the flesh.

Brush the toasted bread slices with oil and the reserved roasted pepper juices. Mix the peppers, tomatoes and flaked tuna together in a bowl, then spoon on to the slices of bread. Top with the herbs, capers and olives.

Drizzle the red wine vinegar and the rest of the extra virgin olive oil over the bread slices, season well with salt and pepper and enjoy!

WHAT TO DRINK

Made famous in Venetian enoteca, but now everywhere, cicchetti are small bites with big flavours. When having fun, the people of the Veneto turn to their favourite bubbly drink – Prosecco! For an extra bit of fun, try Fiol Prosecco Rosé, an innovative yet classic example of Prosecco. This wine blends two grapes Glera and Pinot Noir, with the latter adding both texture and colour. With elegant bubbles, Fiol Prosecco Rosé has notes of raspberries, wild strawberries and citrus followed by a long, persistent finish.

BROAD BEAN PURÉE CICCHETTI

PURÉ DI FAVE

Enjoy this wonderful purée during the very brief, early Summer broad/fava bean season.

500 g/1 lb. 2 oz. podded fresh
   or frozen broad/fava beans
2 garlic cloves, peeled
50 g/2 oz. crustless white bread
about 2 tablespoons milk
5 tablespoons extra virgin olive oil,
   plus extra for drizzling
12-16 slices of ciabatta bread
sea salt and freshly ground
   black pepper

TO GARNISH
fresh mint leaves
grated lemon zest

Serves 6-8

Add the broad beans to a saucepan of simmering water along with one of the garlic cloves. Cook at a low simmer for 5 minutes until the beans are tender. Drain the beans and garlic, reserving 2 tablespoons of the liquid and set aside to cool.

Place the bread in a bowl and pour on enough milk to moisten it.

Slip the broad beans out of their white skins and discard the skins. This will give you a really creamy purée. Put the bright emerald beans, both garlic cloves and the bread with its milk into a food processor. Whiz to a coarse purée, gradually adding the olive oil through the funnel. If the purée is very thick, add a little of the reserved bean cooking liquid. Taste and adjust the seasoning.

Preheat the oven to 180°C/160°C fan/350°F/Gas 4. Bake the ciabatta for 10-12 minutes until crisp and golden. Moisten the bread with a little oil, then serve with the purée and mint leaves and lemon zest to garnish.

Illustrated on page 16.

PROSCIUTTO WITH FRESH FIGS & MOZZARELLA CICCHETTI

PROSCIUTTO CON FICHI FRESCHI E MOZZARELLA

Ripe and flavourful fresh figs are essential to create this delicious plate.

150 g/5 oz. fresh buffalo mozzarella
   cheese
2-3 teaspoons aged balsamic vinegar
2 tablespoons extra virgin olive oil
8 slices of prosciutto
4 slices of bread, toasted
2 ripe, fresh figs, halved vertically
large handful of pine nuts, toasted
sea salt and freshly ground
   black pepper
lemon wedges, to serve (optional)

Serves 4

Tear the fresh buffalo mozzarella into pieces and place in a bowl. Dress the mozzarella with a little aged balsamic vinegar and extra virgin olive oil. Season the mozzarella with a little salt and a generous grinding of black pepper.

Pile 2 slices of prosciutto and some of the dressed mozzarella onto each toasted bread slice and top with half a fresh fig and some toasted pine nuts. Serve with lemon wedges for squeezing over, if liked.

Illustrated on page 20.

CHICKEN LIVER CICCHETTI

FEGATINI DI POLLO

A very old recipe, well worth the effort and it improves with age.
This is rich, elegant and intense.

250 g/9 oz. chicken livers

2 tablespoons olive oil

1 celery stalk/rib, finely chopped

1 shallot, peeled and very finely chopped

2 small garlic cloves, peeled and chopped

generous handful of chopped fresh flat-leaf parsley, plus extra to garnish

125 g/4 oz. lean minced/ground beef

1 tablespoon tomato purée/paste

6 tablespoons dry white wine

12–16 slices of ciabatta bread or day old country bread

1 tablespoon capers, rinsed and chopped

2 salted anchovy fillets, rinsed and finely chopped

100 g/3½ oz. unsalted butter

extra virgin olive oil, to drizzle

sea salt and freshly ground black pepper

Serves 6–8

Trim the fat and gristle from the chicken livers, then rinse, pat dry with kitchen paper and chop finely. Set aside.

Heat the oil in a saucepan over a medium heat. Add the celery, shallot, garlic and parsley. Cook for about 10 minutes until soft, stirring frequently.

Add the chicken livers and beef and cook over a very low heat until the livers have lost their raw colour and become crumbly. Mix in the tomato purée and cook for 1 minute.

Increase the heat, pour in the wine and boil to reduce until almost totally evaporated. Lower the heat and add a little salt and plenty of pepper. Simmer for 30 minutes, adding a little hot water if the mixture becomes too dry.

Meanwhile, preheat the oven to 180°C/160°C fan/350°F/ Gas 4. To make the crostini, bake the ciabatta or country bread slices for 10-12 minutes until crisp and golden.

Add the capers and anchovies to the liver mixture. Mix in the butter and cook gently for 5 minutes, stirring constantly. Moisten the crostini with a little extra virgin olive oil, then spread the chicken liver mixture on top. Sprinkle over a little extra chopped parsley, then serve at once.

SALAD OF APPLE, SPECK & ASIAGO CHEESE

INSALATA PONTORMO

Pontormo was a Renaissance painter who kept a journal of his gastronomic experiments. This recipe is a modern variation of one of his recipes. Speck is a kind of smoked prosciutto available in the northern regions of Italy. Asiago cheese is a semi-hard cheese made from cow's milk – it is delicious and uplifts any dish.

1 red apple
250 g/9 oz. speck or Parma ham
250 g/9 oz. asiago cheese
1 frisée lettuce and 1 bunch lamb's
    lettuce/corn salad, washed
    and trimmed
sea salt and freshly ground
    black pepper

LEMON DRESSING
6 tablespoons extra virgin olive oil
finely grated zest and juice of
    1 unwaxed lemon

Serves 4

First, make the dressing. In a small bowl, whisk together the olive oil, lemon juice and zest.

Core the unpeeled apple and slice very thinly. Cut the speck into thin strips and cut the cheese into small dice.

In a serving bowl, combine the frisée and lamb's lettuce with the apple, speck and cheese. Toss well with the lemon dressing and season with salt and pepper to taste.

RADICCHIO IN SAOR

RADICCHIO IN SAOR

I've grown up safe in the knowledge that radicchio is special, not only for my father's business but as a tasty, health-giving vegetable that is extremely versatile and grows well in the fertile soil of the Veneto and other areas. Please try a crostini with this particular topping.

40 g/¹⁄₃ cup raisins
8 heads of radicchio treviso
2 medium onions
1 tablespoon olive oil
75 ml/¹⁄₃ cup red wine vinegar
30 g/¹⁄₄ cup pine nuts
1 teaspoon sugar
3 tablespoons extra virgin olive oil
sea salt and freshly ground
    black pepper

Serves 4-6

Leave the raisins to steep in a little lukewarm water for 20 minutes.

Wash the radicchio, dry well and cut each into 4 pieces lengthways.

Peel and finely slice the onions, cook in a large pan with the olive oil and cook until it is a lightly coloured. Add the vinegar and then the pine nuts. Next, add the radicchio and continue cooking over a medium heat, stirring now and then, for about 12 minutes. Add the extra virgin olive oil and season well with salt and pepper.

This saor can be served on crostini as cicchetti (you will need to cut the radicchio into smaller pieces to top the crostini) and can also be served as an antipasto.

Illustrated on page 25.

SWEET & SOUR ONIONS

CIPOLLINE IN AGRODOLCE

This is a typical antipasto dish eaten throughout the whole of Italy. It makes a good preserve, covered with olive oil in jars. Of all the dishes I cook at the school, this gets the most compliments. It is also a great way to use up an overabundance of grapes. Nothing could be more delicious and, strangely enough, it is one of my most requested recipes and just happens to be the simplest.

1 dessertspoon caster/
   granulated sugar
15 g/¹⁄₂ oz. butter
2 bay leaves
450 g/1 lb. Italian bortonni onions
   (see Note below) or shallots,
   peeled
50 ml/scant ¹⁄₄ cup white wine
100 g/3¹⁄₂ oz. black grapes, halved
   and deseeded
a handful of fresh flat-leaf parsley,
   chopped (optional)
sea salt and freshly ground
   black pepper
bread, to serve

Serves 4

Heat the sugar in a heavy-based saucepan with a tablespoon of water until it caramelizes and becomes the colour of hay. Immediately stir in the butter and bay leaves.

Toss the onions into this mixture for a couple of minutes, then pour in the wine. Season, bring to the boil, cover and simmer for 20 minutes.

Add the grapes and simmer for a further 10 minutes, with the lid off, to reduce the liquid. Adjust the seasoning and remove the bay leaves.

Pour into a dish and garnish with parsley, if liked. Serve hot or cold with bread for mopping up the delicious juices.

Note: *Bortonni onions are small and flat, similar to a disc in shape. Native to Italy, they can be quite hard to find elsewhere, but shallots or large spring or salad onions/scallions will substitute very well. Shallots and onions (and garlic) all contain sulphurous chemicals called allins, which are responsible for the onion odour (as well as the tears induced by cutting onions). These are believed by traditional medicine to be a tonic, stimulant and diuretic.*

POTATO & GORGONZOLA FOCACCIA

FOCACCIA DI PATATE CON GORGONZOLA

*This is an old favourite of mine. It is so appropriate for the Veneto,
where the Gorgonzola is a gift, that it had to be included here.*

DOUGH

2 medium potatoes, peeled
and chopped

500-550 g (4-4⅓ cups) strong
white bread flour, plus extra
for dusting and kneading

2 teaspoons fine sea salt

15 g/½ oz. fresh yeast, crumbled
or 7 g/¼ oz. active dry yeast

250 ml/1 cup water at body
temperature

3 tablespoons olive oil, plus
extra for greasing

TOPPING

1 x 400-g/14-oz. can Italian plum
tomatoes, drained and chopped

1 tablespoon chopped fresh
oregano

2 tablespoons torn fresh basil

1 garlic clove, finely chopped

½ teaspoon freshly ground
black pepper

375 g/13 oz. quartered artichoke
hearts in olive oil

250 g/9 oz. Gorgonzola cheese,
crumbled

150 g/5½ oz. mozzarella, shredded

extra virgin olive oil, for drizzling

38 x 25 x 2.5-cm (15 x 10 x 1-in.)
rimmed baking sheet

**Serves 8-12 (depending
on the size of your slices)**

Boil the potatoes in a covered saucepan of salted water for
10-15 minutes or until they are tender. Drain and mash them,
then leave to cool slightly.

In a large bowl, mix two thirds of the flour with the salt.
Dissolve the yeast in 2 tablespoons of the water and add it to
a well in the centre of the flour, along with the olive oil. Mix for
a few minutes, then stir in the mashed potatoes and as much
of the remaining flour as you can.

On a lightly floured work surface, knead in enough of the
remaining flour to make a stiff dough that is both smooth and
elastic. This will take about 8–10 minutes. Shape the dough into
a ball and place it in an oiled bowl, turning it once to grease
the entire surface. Cover it with a damp, clean tea towel/
dishcloth and leave it to rise in a warm place for about
1 hour or until it has doubled in size.

Knock back the dough, cover and let it rest for 10 minutes.

Grease the baking sheet and press the dough into it. If it is
sticky, dust the surface with 1 tablespoon of extra flour. Using
your fingertips, make small indentations in the dough. Cover
and leave it to prove for about 30 minutes until it has nearly
doubled in size.

Meanwhile, preheat the oven to 190°C/170°C fan/375°F/Gas 5.

For the topping, mix the tomatoes, oregano, basil, garlic and
black pepper and spoon evenly over the dough. Place the
artichoke hearts over the tomato sauce mixture, then cover
with the gorgonzola and shredded mozzarella. Bake in the hot
oven for 35 minutes until golden. Serve hot, drizzled with the
extra virgin olive oil.

MELON, PROSCIUTTO & ROCKET SALAD

INSALATA DI MELONE CON PROSCIUTTO E RUCOLA

Perfect for a sweltering hot day when a light bite of something sweet and savoury is demanded. Please ensure your melon is at it is peak of perfection – check that it is heavy as a sign that the sugar in the melon has ripened.

2 tablespoons extra virgin olive oil

3/4 tablespoon red wine vinegar

1/2 tablespoon chopped fresh oregano leaves, plus extra to serve

500 g/1 lb. 2 oz. melon, rind removed and thinly sliced (I use Cantaloupe melon)

1/2 red onion, very finely sliced

handful of rocket/arugula, washed

125 g/4 1/2 oz. prosciutto, chopped

sea salt and finely ground black pepper

crusty bread, to serve

Serves 4–6

First, make the dressing. Mix the oil, vinegar and oregano together in a small bowl and season to taste.

Tumble the melon, onion and dressing together and let it all stand for 30 minutes.

Arrange on a plate and top with the rocket, prosciutto and more oregano. Serve with crusty bread to mop up the dressing.

PRAWNS & WHITE BEANS VENETIAN STYLE

GAMBERI CON FAGIOLI ALLA VENEZIANA

Venetians love seafood, and the combination of prawns/shrimp and beans in this delicate salad is delicious.

125 g/4 oz. dried cannellini beans, soaked in cold water overnight

2 rosemary sprigs

3 bay leaves

3 thyme sprigs

3 flat-leaf parsley sprigs

4 garlic cloves, unpeeled

500 g/1 lb. 2 oz. large raw prawns/ shrimp with heads and shells on

2 celery stalks/ribs, finely chopped

juice of 1 lemon

handful of fresh flat-leaf parsley, chopped

2-3 tablespoons extra virgin olive oil

sea salt and freshly ground black pepper

lemon wedges, to serve

Serves 4

Drain the cannellini beans and place in a large saucepan. Add plenty of cold water to cover, and add the herbs and unpeeled garlic. Bring to the boil, then reduce the heat and cook for about 1 1/2 hours or until the beans are tender. Drain the beans and discard the herbs and garlic.

Add the prawns to a saucepan of boiling salted water and simmer for 2 minutes, then drain.

Combine the beans and prawns in a bowl and add the celery, lemon juice and parsley. Season well with salt and pepper, drizzle with extra virgin olive oil and toss to mix. Serve with lemon wedges for squeezing over.

Illustrated on page 33.

SOUP & RISOTTO

ZUPPE E RISOTTI

GO WITH THE GRAIN

The majority of European rice is grown in the great plain carved by the River Po: this plain covers 57 per cent of the region. Most of the rice is used in risotti – more popular here than pasta – and in soups. Both dishes, which are *primi* or first courses, are wonderful springboards for utilizing foodstuffs that are in season (seasonality being one of the major Italian food passions), from seafood to wild mushrooms, from vegetables to game.

Rice cultivation in the Veneto began around the 16th century, encouraged by the Republic of Venice. Because the River Po regularly flooded, making the land marshy, major irrigation systems were built to drain the marshes of their stagnant water, and also to bring fresh spring water back to the fields: rice plants need to have their feet in water. (However, global warming is now a threat to rice and Venetian agriculture in general. Italy suffered its worst ever drought in 2022, and the waters of the Po are at their lowest level for years.)

There are four formal grades of rice grown in Italy: *commune* (common), *semifino* (semi fine), *fino* (fine) and *superfino* (super fine). Arborio and carnaroli are *superfino*, with long grains, while vialone nano is a shorter-grained *semifino*. Other rices are short and round, more like pudding rice.

The primary characteristic of a risotto rice is its ability to release its starch and absorb flavours. Although arborio is the most commonly available, I think vialone nano is the best rice for risotto as it is plumply starchy around the central kernel. The release of this starch, caused by the constant stirring, makes the *crema*, or creaminess, for the best risottos.

I was introduced to rice and risotto fairly late on, as my childhood home was in the south, where pasta reigns supreme. My father, a vegetable and fruit exporter, once took me to a rice festival in Isola della Scala, a municipality of the province of Verona. Held annually in autumn/fall, it is now a wonderful showcase for local produce, and the locally grown vialone nano rice. (Vialone nano – or to give it its proper name, *Riso Nano Vialone Veronese* – is an

IGP food.) Dad and I sat on straw bales and sampled at least five different risottos, including the local *risotto all'Isolana*, which featured minced/ground meat and a touch of cinnamon. My favourite though, was a pumpkin risotto, which had a crispy rice cake balanced on the top to keep it warm.

Other risottos found in Veneto depend on geography. On the plains you might find *risotto primavera*, with young spring vegetables, or the wonderful white asparagus risotto from Vicenza. You would find risottos made with wild mushrooms and game from the forests and mountains, and radicchio recipes from the towns that grow the vegetable. But along the coastlines, and particularly in Venice and its lagoon, you will come across the most famed risottos of Veneto: *risotto al nero di seppia*, cuttlefish cooked with its ink sacs intact, giving the white rice an inky black colour; *risotto alle vongole*, with clams; *risotto al frutte di mare*, with seafood; *risotto di gò*, invented by Burano fishermen centuries ago using goby, an ugly small lagoon fish; and perhaps even a risotto using *rane*, frogs, which thrive in the watery rice paddies - a logical and delicious combination!

There are also specific words associated with risotto making. You start with the *soffritto*, chopped onion, perhaps with celery and carrot, which is cooked in butter or olive oil. When the rice is added, each grain must be 'toasted' or coated well with fat, the *tostatura*. When the risotto is cooked *all'onda*, 'like a wave' (Venetian risottos are more liquid), it is ready. It is then dressed with butter - *mantecatura* - and eaten, when it should be *al dente*, 'to the tooth'.

Both rice and pasta find their place in northern Italian soups. Because of the weather - winters are cold and quite bleak in Veneto - most soups are hearty and warming. Beans, fresh and dried, feature a lot. There are some IGP bean varieties grown in Veneto, among them the *fagioli di Lamon*, a borlotti bean from Belluno. There are bean and pasta soups, as well as bean and rice soups.

Dried beans, and other pulses, are a staple of the store-cupboard, which Italians value, always there for (almost) immediate use. Italians are good at leftovers too, and my *passatelli in brodo* is nothing more complicated than stale breadcrumbs, mixed with Parmesan and egg, shaved into a boiling broth. I first had this in Verona, the *nonna* of the family cooked it for us before we went to church for a wedding.

The most characteristic soup of Veneto, though, is from Venice. *Risi e bisi*, 'rice and peas' in the Venetian dialect, is a soup so thick it resembles a risotto, and is always eaten with a spoon. It is made when the spring peas become available. I remember just holding out my bags to the pea seller and him tipping pods in without even weighing them first! The stock is made from the pods, and the flavour is divinely fresh. The dish was once offered to the Doges, the leaders of Venice, in celebration of Saint Mark, the patron saint of the Republic.

LITTLE BREAD DUMPLINGS IN BROTH

PASSATELLI IN BRODO

I first enjoyed this delicious soup at lunch before my friend Christiana got married.
Her grandmother, Madellena Chapello, a great friend of mine and my father's, prepared it.
Madellena didn't have a ricer, so all the dumplings were hand rolled. This is a light,
nutritious soup, usually served in the home or in trattorias.

55 g/ 2 oz. fresh breadcrumbs

55 g/2 oz. freshly grated Parmesan
cheese, plus extra to serve

freshly grated nutmeg, to taste

1 large egg, beaten

850 ml/1½ pints vegetable stock

good handful of fresh flat-leaf
parsley, chopped

sea salt and freshly ground
black pepper

freshly torn basil, to garnish

Serves 4

To prepare the dumplings, on a large board, mix together the
breadcrumbs, Parmesan, nutmeg and some salt and pepper
to taste. Make a well in the centre, add the beaten egg and
knead for about 3 minutes. Set aside and rest in the fridge
for 20 minutes.

Pour the stock into a large saucepan set over a medium
heat. Add the parsley and bring to a slow boil.

Ensure that the dumpling mixture is slack enough to be pressed
through a ricer, if not add a little water. Pass the mixture through
a ricer directly into the boiling stock. The dumplings will be
ready as soon as they float to the surface in the delicious broth.
Top with extra Parmesan and basil to serve.

Note: *To roll the dumplings by hand, pull off tiny amounts of dough
and hand-roll into tiny sausage shapes, about the size of your little
finger and cook as instructed above.*

VEGETABLE SOUP WITH RICE & BEANS

MINESTRONE CON RISO E FAGIOLI

In Italy there are a multitude of vegetable soups or minestrone – roughly translated, the word means a 'mixture' or 'hotchpotch'. It is a dish typical of the north, where people need fuel and energy for the colder weather.

1 tablespoon olive oil

2 garlic cloves, chopped

1 celery stalk/rib, finely chopped

1 red onion, sliced

8 ripe, fresh, red tomatoes, skinned

500 g/18 oz. cooked borlotti beans

200 g/7 oz. arborio risotto rice

1/2 teaspoon dried chilli/hot red pepper
   flakes

handful of fresh flat-leaf parsley, chopped

handful of fresh mint, chopped

sea salt and freshly ground
   black pepper

extra virgin olive oil, for drizzling

Serves 4

Heat the olive oil in a saucepan over a medium heat. Add the garlic, celery and onion and sauté until softened. Add the tomatoes and simmer for 10 minutes.

Add the cooked beans to the saucepan, then add the rice and 450 ml/1¾ cups water, stirring well. Add the chilli flakes, parsley and mint and cook for 20 minutes until the rice is tender. You may need to add more water if the soup is too thick. Season with salt and pepper and serve with a drizzle of extra virgin olive oil.

WHAT TO DRINK

This dish is just asking for a fruity red with a bit of spice. What better than a Valpolicella DOC Classico? Try Le Salette by the winery of the same name. The grapes are hand picked at their peak flavour and have no aging in oak, resulting in a dry red with an abundance of ripe cherries, herbs and liquorice balanced with good acidity and a clean finish. This wine offers depth to complement the mix of flavours in the dish.

BEAN & CABBAGE SOUP

JOTA

This northern dish is eaten for *pranzo* (lunch) with a hunk of bread during the winter months. It's almost mandatory for all Italians to eat lots of beans during the winter as they believe them to be synonymous with health, warmth and energy. I recommend you make this soup the day before you plan to eat it.

350 g/12½ oz. cooked cannellini beans
   (see page 46)

1 medium fennel bulb, chopped

1 onion, chopped

2 garlic cloves, crushed

1 green cabbage, shredded

4 tablespoons tomato purée/paste

2 tablespoons olive oil

handful of fresh flat-leaf parsley, chopped

sea salt and freshly ground black pepper

Serves 4

When the beans have nearly finished their cooking, stir in the fennel, onion, garlic, cabbage, tomato purée and season with salt and pepper. Simmer for 30 minutes or until the beans are tender.

Add the olive oil and parsley, then taste and adjust the seasoning before serving.

Note: *Cabbage contains Vitamins A, B and C; the darker the colour of the leaves, the higher the content of nutrients.*

FISH SOUP WITH MACARONI

ZUPPA DI PESCE E MACCHERONCINI

Every trattoria, the length and breadth of the coastline of Italy, will serve
a fish soup like this – perfectly plain, pure and simple.

250 g/9 oz. boneless monkfish steaks

250 g/9 oz. boneless cod steaks

250 g/9 oz. boneless sea bass fillets

generous handful of fresh flat-leaf
parsley, finely chopped

2 tablespoons olive oil

1 medium onion, chopped

2 garlic cloves, chopped

1 x 400-g/14-oz. can chopped
tomatoes

200 g/7 oz. macaroni

sea salt and freshly ground
black pepper

Serves 4

Cut the fish into fork-friendly chunks,

Bring 2.25 litres/2⅓ quarts cold water to the boil. Reduce the heat, add the fish chunks and one-third of the parsley and simmer for about 10 minutes. Transfer the fish to a plate using a slotted spoon, then strain and reserve the cooking liquid.

Combine the olive oil, onion, garlic, tomatoes and half the remaining parsley in a clean saucepan. Season with salt and pepper and simmer gently for 10 minutes.

Add the reserved fish broth and the macaroni to the pan and cook gently until the pasta is done, tasting as you go.

Add the fish to the pan and heat through briefly. Sprinkle with the remaining parsley and serve hot.

FISH BROTH

ZUPPA DI PESCE

Broth (or stock) or *brodo* is the foundation of most soups and sauces. The role of broth in Italian cuisine dates back to Roman times and broth and soups in general have traditionally been used to strengthen up the weak or ill. Societies long ago also learned the value of making broths to lend richness and depth of flavour to their dishes. Fish broth is easy to make – use all your seafood carcasses and bones from white fish for the most flavoursome result, but avoid using oily fish.

1 kg/2 lb. 4 oz. white fish
and/or seafood carcasses

3 fresh bay leaves

1 celery stalk/rib

1 carrot

2 onions

1 fresh parsley stalk

Makes about 750ml/3 cups

Toss all the ingredients into a large stockpot or saucepan with 1 litre/4 cups water and boil for 25 minutes.

Leave to cool and then strain the liquid into a bowl.

This broth will keep in the fridge for up to 3 days.

PASTA & BEANS

PASTA E FAGIOLI

This famous soup must, according to my grandmother, be served hot with a 'C' of extra virgin olive oil trickled over the surface. Foolishly, I never found out why! The original recipe advises cooking the beans in an earthenware pot in a slow oven for 3 hours. I find, however, that excellent results are obtained if the recipe is streamlined and adapted to modern rhythms: cooked and ready to serve in an hour and a half. Italian soups are not as liquid as those elsewhere, so don't worry if it looks a little thick.

A high-carbohydrate and high-energy dish, especially perfect for winter, it uses virtually no oil. Other pulses/legumes could be used in this recipe in place of the cannellini beans. It's so versatile, you'll soon be able to put your own stamp on the recipe.

300 g/11 oz. dried cannellini
   beans, or 2 x 400-g/14-oz.
   cans cooked beans
1 sage sprig
1 rosemary sprig
1 garlic clove, crushed
dried chilli/hot red pepper flakes,
   to taste
200 g/7 oz. rigatoni pasta
   (short, ribbed tubes)
sea salt and freshly ground
   black pepper

TO SERVE
extra virgin olive oil
freshly grated Parmesan

Serves 6

Soak the dried beans in water for 24 hours. Drain, cover with fresh water and a lid and bring to the boil for 10 minutes. Thereafter, cook over a gentle heat for 40 minutes, along with the herbs and garlic to lend flavour and aroma.

If using canned beans, simply drain and rinse, add the herbs and garlic, then just cover with cold water and heat through for about 20 minutes. Top up with more water as necessary.

Push the beans and liquid through a sieve/strainer to eliminate the tough outer husks, then place the purée in a saucepan. Season with salt and pepper and a little pinch of chilli flakes to taste.

Add the pasta to the bean purée with 4 tablespoons water and cook, stirring occasionally to prevent the pasta sticking, until the pasta is cooked to your liking.

To serve, drizzle the hot soup with extra virgin olive oil and scatter over Parmesan to taste.

Note: *Pasta cooking time can be affected by so many things - the size of pan you use, quality of pan you use, how vigorously the water is boiling, how much salt you have added, type and quality of pasta used - so I always say it is best to regularly check your pasta as it is cooking until it reaches the perfect level of doneness, rather than giving a firm time to follow.*

RISOTTO WITH PEAS
RISI E BISI

This recipe has become a speciality of Venice because of the wonderful soil of the Veneto where peas grow in abundance. During the pea season, there is often such a glut that the vendors don't bother to weigh them out but just pour the pods freely into your bag, so as to ensure that you can enjoy them at their very finest and sweetest. There are very, very many variations of this dish. I've studied the variations and am delighted to share this recipe for you to enjoy.

50 g/3½ tablespoons unsalted butter
2 tablespoons olive oil
6 shallots, finely sliced
2 garlic cloves, finely chopped
handful of fresh flat-leaf parsley, chopped
1 kg/2 lb. 4 oz. young fresh pea pods, shelled and rinsed
1 litre/4 cups hot vegetable stock (preferably home-made)
350 g/12 oz. vialone nano risotto rice
125 ml/½ cup dry white wine
handful of fresh mint, chopped
55 g/2 oz. freshly grated Parmesan, plus extra to serve
sea salt and freshly ground black pepper

Serves 4

Heat the butter and oil in a frying pan/skillet over a medium heat and fry the shallots and garlic until lightly coloured.

Stir in the parsley, peas and just enough hot stock to barely cover the ingredients. Simmer gently for 2 minutes.

Add the rice, wine and some black pepper and stir to coat the rice with this mixture, using a wooden spoon.

Add the stock, ladleful by ladleful, stirring well between each addition, until all the stock has been absorbed and the rice is creamy. This should take about 18-20 minutes.

Stir in some salt, and then the mint and Parmesan. Remove the pan from the heat, cover and leave for 1 minute to allow the rice to rest. Serve on warmed plates or bowls with extra grated Parmesan, if desired.

Note: *Because they are green, peas contain rich supplies of Vitamin A and C. They are a stimulant and supply energy. Peas should be eaten as fresh as possible because, once plucked from the plant, their sugars rapidly convert to starch.*

SEAFOOD RISOTTO

RISOTTO AI FRUTTI DI MARE

The very best risotto undoubtedly comes from the Veneto, where seafood is in abundance. We Italians like to serve our risotto all'onda meaning 'like a wave in the sea'. Risotti is at home in the north of Italy, as a rule of thumb. Southern rice dishes are very disappointing.

750 ml/3 cups home-made
   fish broth (see page 45)
150 ml/²/₃ cup dry white wine
125 g/4¹/₂ oz. monkfish, cut into
   2-cm/³/₄-inch cubes
300 g/10¹/₂ oz. large raw prawns/
   shrimp, with heads and shells on
4 queen scallops, halved
4 fresh squid, cleaned and
   cut into strips
250 g/9 oz. mussels, cleaned
125 g/4¹/₂ oz. clams
2 tablespoons olive oil
3 shallots, finely chopped
225 g/8 oz. carnaroli risotti rice
1 garlic clove, finely chopped
handful of flat-leaf parsley,
   chopped
sea salt and freshly ground
   black pepper

Serves 4-6

Heat the broth and wine together in a large pan over a medium heat for a few minutes. Add the monkfish, prawns, scallops and squid and cook for 4 minutes. Remove the monkfish and seafood and set aside.

Add the mussels and clams to the hot stock and cook for about 4 minutes until the shells have opened. Remove the clams and mussels with a slotted spoon. Discard any that have not opened.

The stock will have oceans of flavour and can be very concentrated so be mindful that it can be topped up with hot water, if needed, to complete the cooking of the rice. Keep the stock warm ready to make the risotto.

Heat the oil in a frying pan/skillet, add the shallots and cook until translucent. Add the rice and stir-fry the grains and shallot mixture until golden and the rice is slightly nutty. Add the garlic and mix well.

Add the hot stock in ladlefuls, continuously stirring with a wooden spoon until all the liquid has been absorbed. Repeat this process until the rice is tender, but there is a tiny bit of chalkiness still in the rice.

Return all the beautiful fish and seafood to the pan and mix very well, loyally topping up with the stock until the risotto is *all'onda*. The risotto should move like the parting of the waves in the ocean.

Spoon the risotto into warmed serving bowls and sprinkle with parsley to serve.

VEAL & MUSHROOM RISOTTO WITH MASCARPONE & BASIL

RISOTTO DI VITELLO CON FUNGHI, MASCARPONE E BASILICO

A dreamy combination of ingredients I first enjoyed in Verona with my father on one of our infamous busy trips. Please do try making your own mascarpone, you will be pleasantly surprised.

10 g/½ oz. dried porcini
  mushrooms
1 litre/4 cups simmering chicken
  broth or vegetable broth
2 tablespoons olive oil
10 g/2 teaspoons unsalted butter
3 shallots, finely chopped
185 g/6½ oz. veal scallops,
  cut into thin strips
1 medium tomato, peeled,
  deseeded and chopped
380 g/13½ oz. arborio risotto rice
150 ml/⅔ cup dry white wine
2 tablespoons fresh mascarpone
  cheese (see page 181)
generous handfuls of torn basil
  leaves, plus extra to serve
2 tablespoons freshly grated
  Parmesan, plus extra to serve
sea salt and freshly ground
  black pepper

Serves 4

Cover the porcini mushrooms with cold water in a small bowl and set aside for 25 minutes to soften. Strain the porcini liquid into the simmering broth, then chop the dried porcini and set aside.

Heat a frying pan/skillet with the oil and butter, add the shallots and cook for about 5 minutes until gently softened.

Add the veal and tomato and cook gently for 5 minutes until the meat changes from pink to pale brown, and then season with black pepper.

Add the rice to the pan with the veal and stir well, coating the rice and mixing the meat and porcini together. Add the wine, stirring well until the wine has evaporated.

Now, start adding the hot broth, a ladleful at a time, stirring continuously and making sure the rice has absorbed each addition and starts to swell. Cook the rice until it is al dente.

Add the mascarpone, basil and Parmesan and season to taste. Leave the risotto to stand for 4 minutes before serving in warmed serving bowls. Check for seasoning and sprinkle with a little extra Parmesan and fresh basil. Enjoy.

RISOTTO WITH COURGETTES & MOZZARELLA

RISOTTO CON ZUCCHINE E MOZZARELLA

For the warm Summer months, I can think of nothing nicer to eat.

2 tablespoons olive oil

1 large garlic clove, crushed

500 g/1 lb. 2 oz. courgettes/
zucchini, cut into matchsticks

3 shallots, finely chopped

225 g/8 oz. arborio or carnaroli
risotto rice

150 ml/²/₃ cup dry white wine

750 ml/3 cups hot vegetable broth
(preferably home-made)

125 g/4¹/₂ oz. mozzarella cheese,
cut into tiny cubes

125 g/4¹/₂ oz. Parmesan, grated

handful of freshly torn basil

extra virgin olive oil, to serve

Serves 4

Combine half the olive oil and the garlic in a sauté pan and fry gently until softened. Add the courgettes and cook over a medium heat for 8–10 minutes until the courgettes are tender. Season with salt and pepper and set aside.

Heat the rest of the olive oil in a separate sauté pan, add the shallots and cook gently until translucent.

When the shallots are translucent, add the rice and mix together very well. Cook until the rice is nutty.

Add the wine and cook to reduce the liquid and the rice starts to swell in the pan.

Add ladlefuls of hot broth and stir the rice with a wooden spoon until each addition has been absorbed. Repeat the process continually until all the stock has been absorbed. This should take about 18 minutes but do taste the rice. It should have a slight chalkiness between the teeth.

Once this has been achieved, add the cooked courgettes, mozzarella, Parmesan and seasoning. Stir everything together, cover, and then leave the risotto to stand for 3 minutes.

Serve the risotto in warmed serving bowls and scattered with extra Parmesan, basil leaves and a drizzle of extra virgin olive oil.

MONKFISH & ASPARAGUS RISOTTO WITH LEMON THYME BUTTER

RISOTTO CON CODA DI ROSPO ED ASPARAGI

Do use the tail of the monkfish for this dish; ask your fishmonger to remove the membrane from the tail as this can be a bit tricky. This risotto is popular with my family and husband who have an aversion to fish bones.

750 ml/3 cups hot vegetable stock (preferably home-made)

8 new season asparagus spears, sliced diagonally, reserve the woody stems for the broth

1½ tablespoons olive oil

50 g/3½ tablespoons unsalted butter

4 shallots, finely chopped

225 g/1⅛ cups carnaroli risotto rice

600 g/1 lb. 6 oz. monkfish tails (see recipe introduction)

fresh lemon thyme leaves, to garnish

LEMON THYME BUTTER

50 g/3½ tablespoons unsalted butter, softened

generous handful of fresh lemon thyme leaves, roughly chopped

1 small garlic clove, finely chopped

grated zest of 1 unwaxed lemon

a baking sheet lined with parchment paper

Serves 4

To make the lemon thyme butter, mix the ingredients together in a bowl, then mould into a log shape and wrap in cling film/plastic wrap. Chill until firm.

Heat the stock in a saucepan, add the woody asparagus stems and cook for 8-10 minutes until the stems start to yield and are tender.

In a wide based pan, heat the oil and butter and gently fry the shallots until golden. Add the rice and continue to stir for 2 minutes. Start adding a ladleful of stock at a time to the rice and stir well between each addition. Repeat this process until the rice is al dente, then stir in the asparagus spears.

Meanwhile, preheat the oven to 180°C/160°C fan/350°F/ Gas 4.

Season the monkfish tails and place them on the prepared baking sheet. Add some of the lemon thyme butter on top and bake in the hot oven for 12 minutes.

When the risotto is cooked (this should be after about 15 minutes), add the sliced monkfish and stir once gently.

Spoon into warmed shallow serving bowls and top with the remaining lemon thyme butter. Scatter with some fresh lemon thyme leaves and serve.

PASTA, POLENTA & GNOCCHI

PASTA, POLENTA E GNOCCHI

SUSTENANCE IN ABUNDANCE

The north of Italy has become known as the 'polenta, rice and bean belt'. Maize (for polenta) and rice (for risotto) are crops almost exclusively grown in the north, and beans are equally important in the local diet. Wheat for pasta is a major product of the north as well, although pasta is not so popular here as it is further south. But because pasta and polenta are both made from grains, I am marrying them together here, along with gnocchi.

Grains have constituted the food of Italy's rural poor for many centuries, made into sustaining breads, soups and porridges/oatmeals. Before the discovery of the New World in the 16th century, the grains grown would have included wheat, millet and buckwheat. But when maize was introduced to Europe by Christopher Columbus, the Italians took to it immediately. Maize grew happily in the fertile northern plain, it was a fairly problem-free crop, and when its grains were dried and ground, it made 'polenta' – which has become a sustaining and much-loved staple, particularly in the Veneto.

In Italy, polenta is known as *farina gialla* ('yellow flour') or *granturco*, which translates as 'Turkish grain'. (This dates from the 1500s, when maize was newly introduced: everyone thought that anything new could only come from the mysterious country of Turkey...) Maize flour comes as very coarse, medium and fine. (The coarser the flour, the yellower it is.) A white flour is also made in Veneto, from a white corn, *biancaperla* ('white pearl'); this is finer in texture and more delicate in flavour than yellow polenta.

There is an Italian saying that truly sums up the significance of polenta to the people of northern Italy: *'La polenta e utile per quattro cose: serve da minestra, serve da pane, sazia, e scalda le mani.'* ('Polenta is good in four ways: for soup, for bread, for filling one up and for warming the hands.') I don't know about the latter, but I do remember a cold, dank and foggy February day in Venice: my mother and I had soft polenta with a wonderful sauce for lunch, and we were warm all afternoon!

The northern Italians are so fond of their polenta that the pasta-eating southerners have a somewhat derogatory name for them, *polentoni*, (polenta-eaters). And this is the common perception of many to the ubiquity of polenta. Even my husband Richard, not long after we married, queried worriedly whether he would have to eat polenta if we ran out of fresh food. I think he has come round now, for of course, made well with broth, butter and cheese, a potentially bland dish is elevated to a completely new level. And it is gluten-free!

Polenta is traditionally cooked in a large copper pan called a *paiolo*, and stirred with a long wooden

paddle, a *tarai*. It takes about 40 minutes of almost constant stirring. Fortunately, there is a speedier form, instant polenta, which cooks in under 10 minutes. Serve soft polenta, creamy and thick – *como la seta* ('like silk') – with meat, game, poultry or fish. As well as butter and cheese, you could add flavourings, such as herbs. Vicenza is reputed to be the best place to have *polenta e baccalà* (with dried cod), or *polenta e osèi* (with tiny birds). Or the soft, flavoured polenta can be poured into a suitable tray or dish and left to set, then cut into shapes and fried or grilled as an accompaniment to meat or fish, or as the base of a *cicchetto*. My daughter, Antonia, loves polenta chips!

Polenta flour can be used in the coating of thin cuts of meat or fish to be fried. And it can appear in sweet dishes too. Replace some of the flour with polenta in many cakes, and you will have a slightly grainier, moister texture.

Pasta may not be as popular in the north as in the south, but the Veneto has several pasta specialities worth trying. Bigoli are large, fat, spaghetti shapes, with a hole in the middle. Wholewheat is traditional, but 99 per cent of the populace eat white bigoli,

made with '00' flour and eggs (once duck eggs). Bigoli are used in one of Venice's most famous dishes, *bigoli in salsa*, with an anchovy sauce, but can also be used instead of spaghetti with clams, *alle vongole*, another famed local recipe. Pappardelle or tagliatelle are pasta ribbons that are popular in the Veneto, usually served with game sauces in Trentino, with fish in Venice. I use linguine here, but the other pasta ribbons would be equally good with cuttlefish and its ink.

Gargati pasta comes from the Veneto too; its name means 'throat' in the local dialect. It is short cut, with ridged edges and a hole through the middle. It is made from '00' flour and semolina, egg, butter and milk. Gargati are usually served with duck or offal sauces. They, like other smaller pasta shapes, could be used in traditional pasta soups. Casunziei is a fresh filled pasta, in a half-moon shape, popular in the mountainous north. (The name comes from Ladin, a Romance language spoken in parts of northern Italy, particularly Belluno.)

Gnocchi can be made from potato, wheat flour or polenta, with ingredients such as pumpkin, spinach and cheese. Those made with potato are traditional in the Veneto, served with vegetable, meat or cheese sauces, as is pasta. Gnocchi star in the Verona Carnival in February, being served on *Venerdì Gnocolar* ('Gnocchi Friday'). Gnocchi are usually served as a *primo*, first course, but can also accompany main-plate meats or fish. There is even a sweet gnoccho, served with cinnamon butter and sugar, which is a carnival dish in Verona and Venice.

VENETIAN PASTA WITH DUCK
BIGOLI IN SALSA DI ANATRA

Since 1573, the Feast of the Sacrea Rosary has been celebrated in every village and town in the northeastern region of Italy on the 7th of October. The following recipe has always served as its traditional dish. Bigoli (Venetian pasta) is long and thick. It was originally made with buckwheat flour, but in most instances nowadays it is made with '00' flour or semolina.

At one time the bigoli were made with duck eggs, which are larger than those of chickens and serve as a better binding agent. Because duck eggs are largely unavailable, this is an adapted version that is more than adequate. Bigoli has a very satisfying mouthfeel and the ability to absorb rich sauces well. It's quite wonderful.

PASTA
300 g/2¼ cups Italian '00' flour, plus extra for dusting
3 large/US extra large eggs
30 ml/2 tablespoons melted unsalted butter
60 ml/¼ cup milk (you may need a little less)

SAUCE
100 g/½ cup/1 stick unsalted butter
2 tablespoons olive oil
450 g/1 lb. skinless duck breast
1 tablespoon tomato purée/paste
3 garlic cloves, finely chopped
3 generous handfuls of fresh flat-leaf parsley
sea salt and freshly ground black pepper

Serves 6

First make the pasta, heap the flour onto a clean work surface (wooden is best), make a well in the centre and add the eggs, melted butter and milk. Using a fork, begin beating the egg mixture only until it falls off the fork in a fine string. Start working the egg mixture into the flour – slowly but surely a dough will form, but some flour may remain. You are looking for a soft springy dough with a damp texture like clay. Set the dough aside in the fridge for 10 minutes to relax.

Pinch off a marble-sized piece of dough. On a lightly floured surface, roll the dough between your palms to form a long rope about 5 mm/¼ inch thick. Cut the rope into 30-cm/12-inch lengths. Continue rolling and cutting until all the pasta dough is used. Leave the bigoli to dry on a floured surface for 20 minutes.

To make the sauce, heat the butter and oil in a sauté pan set over a medium heat. Cook the duck for 4 minutes on each side, remove and cut the meat into slices.

Return the duck to the pan, add the tomato purée, garlic, 100 ml/scant ½ cup water and some salt and pepper and gently cook, stirring constantly.

Meanwhile, bring a saucepan of salted water to the boil, then add the bigoli and cook for about 8 minutes until al dente.

Drain the pasta and add to the pan with the duck. Mix well, scatter in the parsley, then serve immediately.

LINGUINE WITH CUTTLEFISH INK

LINGUINE AL NERO DI SEPPIA

I find this dish to be extremely light and fresh. It is a touch dramatic being black, however
it will win over even the most sceptical diner with the distinctive briny taste of the squid.

400 g/14 oz. small cuttlefish
and a few ink sacs

2 tablespoons olive oil

1 garlic clove, finely chopped

2 onions, chopped

2 tablespoons dry white wine

5 ripe tomatoes, skinned and
deseeded

400 g/14 oz. dried linguine

pinch of dried chilli/hot red pepper
flakes

1 tablespoon extra virgin olive oil

bunch of fresh flat-leaf parsley,
chopped

sea salt and freshly ground
black pepper

Serves 4-6

Wash the cuttlefish and then roughly chop them into even pieces.

Heat the oil in a saucepan and gently cook the garlic until lightly
coloured. Add the onions and cook until lightly coloured, then add the
cuttlefish, a ladleful of hot water and the white wine. Cook for a further
10 minutes, then add the chopped tomatoes.

Once the sauce has thickened, break the ink sacs into the pan.

Meanwhile, bring a saucepan of salted water to the boil, then add the
linguini and cook for about 8 minutes until al dente, testing as you go.

Drain the pasta and add to the pan with the cuttlefish. Add some chilli
flakes and season to taste. Add the extra virgin olive oil and plenty of
parsley, then serve immediately.

Note: *The pasta used in these recipes are all interchangeable - use bigoli
if you can get it (or make it yourself) or use either linguine or spaghetti.*

SPAGHETTI WITH CLAMS

SPAGHETTI CON VONGOLE IN BIANCO

An iconic recipe, celebrated throughout the coastal regions and much cherished.

1 kg/2 lb. 4 oz. clams

2 tablespoons olive oil

1 fat garlic clove, finely chopped

1 teaspoon dried chilli/
hot red pepper flakes

handful of fresh flat-leaf parsley

400 g/14 oz. dried spaghetti or
linguine

sea salt and freshly ground
black pepper

Serves 4-6

Wash the clams in several changes of water to get rid of any grit. Place
them in a saucepan with enough water to cover. Cover the pan with a
lid and set over a high heat. Once the clams have opened, remove the
pan from the heat and set aside for the clams to cool in the water.
Discard any that have not opened. Strain, reserving the cooking water.

Heat the olive oil in a frying pan/skillet over a medium heat and cook
the garlic until softened. Add the clams, chilli flakes and half the parsley.

Pour the reserved cooking water into a saucepan and bring to the boil.
Add the pasta and cook for about 8 minutes or until al dente. Drain
the pasta, reserving a little of the cooking water in case you need to
loosen the pasta. Add the pasta to the pan with the clams and mix
well. Season and scatter in the remaining parsley to serve.

Illustrated on page 69.

SPAGHETTI WITH ANCHOVIES

SPAGHETTI IN SALSA CON ACCIUGHE

This is considered one of the signature pasta dishes of the Veneto. Originating within the Jewish community in Venice, in times gone by, the sauce was made with salt-cured fish, however, today mainly anchovies are used. When I want a meal that really packs a full flavour punch, this really hits the spot. I love the simplicity of this dish, but sadly my husband does not share my enthusiasm for anchovies and so I only share this recipe when I am teaching at Cison in Venice.

2 tablespoons olive oil

2 onions, finely chopped

50 ml/¼ cup white wine

125 g/4½ oz. salted anchovies
   (more if preferred)

400 g/14 oz. dried spaghetti
   or linguine

extra virgin olive oil, to serve
   (make sure it is very fruity)

handful of fresh flat-leaf parsley,
   roughly chopped, to serve

freshly ground black pepper

Serves 4–6

Heat the olive oil in a saucepan over a medium heat. When hot, add the onions and gently cook for at least 15 minutes until the onions are soft, golden and yielding.

Add the white wine and cook until the liquid has evaporated. Add the anchovies (you can adjust the amount according to your taste), stir through the onions and cook for 6 minutes.

Meanwhile, bring a saucepan of salted water to the boil, then add the pasta and cook for about 8 minutes until al dente, testing as you go.

Drain the pasta and add to the pan with the anchovies, then mix well to coat the pasta - it should be rich and silky.

Drizzle over a good few glugs of extra virgin olive oil, scatter some chopped parsley on top and season with plenty of black pepper before serving.

Note: *Always use the best quality anchovies that you can afford - they really will give the dish the best result.*

RAVIOLI WITH CRAB

RAVIOLI AL GRANCHIO

I first enjoyed this ravioli with crab in Venice – indisputably the home of the finest crab in Italy. It makes a super dinner party dish and is relatively straightforward. You can use all white crab meat or a mixture of white and dark. If you use dark meat, the flavour will obviously be much stronger.

½ quantity of fresh
    pasta dough
    (see page 65)
flour, for dusting
90 g/3¼ oz. unsalted
    butter
juice of 1 lemon

FILLING
175 g/6 oz. mascarpone
    cheese (see page 181
    for home-made)

175 g/6 oz. crab meat
    (see recipe intro)
handful of fresh flat-leaf
    parsley, chopped,
    plus extra to serve
finely grated zest of
    1 unwaxed lemon
sea salt and freshly
    ground black pepper

Serves 4

First, make the filling. Put the mascarpone in a bowl and mash well with a fork. Add the crab meat, parsley and lemon zest, along with some salt and pepper to taste. Stir well.

Using a pasta machine, roll out half the dough into a 90–100-cm/36–40-inch strip. With a sharp knife, cut the strip into four 45–50-cm/ 18–20-inch lengths (you can do this during the rolling if the strip gets too long to manage). Use a 8-cm/3-inch round cookie cutter to cut out 8 discs from each pasta strip (or hand-cut if preferred).

Using a teaspoon, put a mound of filling in the centre of half the discs. Brush a little water around the edge of the filled discs, then top each with another disc and press the edges to seal, trying to eliminate as much trapped air as you can. Press the edges with the tines of a fork for decoration.

Put the ravioli on a floured dish or tray lined with baking parchment, sprinkle lightly with flour and leave to dry while repeating the process with the remaining dough and filling.

Bring a large saucepan of salted water to the boil, then add the ravioli. Bring it back to the boil, then reduce the heat and gently poach the ravioli on a low simmer for 4–5 minutes.

Meanwhile, melt the butter with the lemon juice in a small pan until sizzling. Drain the ravioli and divide them equally between warmed bowls. Drizzle the lemon butter over the ravioli, scatter with parsley and serve.

RADICCHIO LASAGNE
LASAGNE DI RADICCHIO ALLA TREVISANA

I have a tremendous love for radicchio, having watched it being grown by my father. From planting to harvest is six weeks, so it is a good vegetable to grow at home. There are two varieties; the round, which is the most common and the Treviso, which is long and thin. Do try to get the Treviso – order it from your greengrocer – as it is much less bitter and much more flavourful.

A friend told me that soaking radicchio for half an hour removes much of it's bitterness. However, it is this very bitterness that most Italians crave, believing that it is a stimulant of the liver, the organ which is the cornerstone of good health.

3 heads of Treviso radicchio

3 tablespoons olive oil

1 medium fennel bulb, trimmed and quartered

300 g/10½ oz. dried lasagne verdi (green pasta sheets)

85 g/⅓ cup unsalted butter

1 onion, finely chopped

55 g/⅓ cup plain/all-purpose flour

1 garlic clove, crushed

500 ml/2 cups whole/full-fat milk

sea salt and freshly ground black pepper

150 g/5½ oz. Gorgonzola cheese, cut into cubes

Serves 4

Preheat the oven to 200°C/180°C fan/400°F/Gas 6.

Quarter the radicchio, wash well and pat dry. Place on a baking sheet and drizzle over the olive oil. Bake in the preheated oven for 10 minutes. The radicchio will change colour and become slightly charred; this will produce the best flavour. Set aside.

Meanwhile, steam the fennel pieces over a pan of boiling water for about 12 minutes until slightly al dente. Once cool enough to handle, finely chop the fennel.

Cook the lasagne sheets in a saucepan of rolling, boiling, salted water until al dente. Drain and set aside.

Next, make the sauce. Melt the butter in a saucepan over a low heat, add the onion and cook until soft and golden. Add the flour, garlic and steamed fennel and cook for a few minutes to remove the raw taste from the flour. Add the milk and some salt and pepper, remove from the heat and stir vigorously with a wooden spoon.

Place the pan back on the heat and bring to the boil, stirring continuously, until the sauce has thickened. Add the cubed Gorgonzola cheese and stir well. Taste to check the seasoning.

To assemble the dish, place a layer of sauce in an ovenproof dish followed by a layer of radicchio and a layer of pasta. Repeat these layers until all the radicchio and pasta have been used up. Finish with any remaining sauce on top.

Place in the preheated oven (still the same temperature as above) and bake for 20 minutes until golden.

TAGLIATELLE WITH SCALLOPS

TAGLIATELLE CON CAPESANTE

Buy fresh scallops with their coral, if possible; they always have a better texture and flavour than frozen scallops, which are very watery. Diver-caught scallops are of a higher quality than the more common dredged ones – you can usually tell the latter as their shells are more likely to be scraped and damaged.

200 g/7 oz. scallops, each sliced across into 2 discs (remove the coral if preferred)

2 tablespoons plain/all-purpose flour

50 g/3½ tablespoons unsalted butter

1 small onion, finely chopped

1 small fresh red chilli/chile, deseeded and very finely chopped

2 tablespoons freshly chopped flat-leaf parsley

4 tablespoons brandy

100 ml/scant ½ cup fish stock (see page 45 for home-made)

350 g/12 oz. tagliatelle

sea salt and freshly ground black pepper

Serves 4

Toss the scallops in the flour, then shake off the excess.

Bring a saucepan of salted water to the boil ready for cooking the tagliatelle.

Meanwhile, melt the butter in a saucepan over a medium heat. Add the onion, chilli and half the parsley and fry, stirring frequently, for 1-2 minutes. Add the scallops and toss over the heat for 1-2 minutes.

Pour the brandy over the scallops and immediately (and carefully) set it alight with a match. As soon as the flames have died down, stir in the fish stock, then season with salt and pepper to taste. Mix well, simmer for 2-3 minutes, then cover the pan and remove it from the heat.

Add the tagliatelle to the boiling water and cook until al dente (just tender but still firm to the bite).

Drain the pasta, add to the sauce and toss over a medium heat until well mixed. Serve immediately, sprinkling over the remaining parsley to finish.

POLENTA WITH SKEWERED MEATS

POLENTA E OSÈI

It's a true sign of friendship to eat this dish as a sharing platter. *Osèi* means 'small birds' in Italian, but not in the tradition of this dish. Emulating the birds, pork, beef and veal have been substituted. Traditionally, this dish would be served with the skewers of meat standing upright, having been stuck into the mound of polenta. It is rather excellent served with sautéed greens.

250 g/9 oz. beef fillet
500 g/1 lb. 2 oz. pork loin fillet
250 g/9 oz. veal escalopes
250 g/9 oz. sliced pancetta
12 fresh sage leaves
4 fennel sausages, casings removed and cut into chunks
500 g/3^1/$_3$ cups coarse polenta/cornmeal
50 g/3^1/$_2$ tablespoons unsalted butter
500 ml/2 cups meat broth
handful of freshly chopped flat-leaf parsley
sea salt and freshly ground black pepper

12 metal skewers, not too long

Serves 4–6

Start with one large piece of each meat, layer it with pancetta and sage, then roll into a log. Slice that log into smaller, fork-friendly chunks, then thread onto the skewers, alternating with chunks of sausage.

Make the basic polenta according to the instructions on page 83, but do not bake it.

While the polenta is cooling, heat the butter in a large frying pan/skillet or sauté pan over a low-medium heat. Add the skewers to the pan and cook for a few minutes on each side until golden. Season well and continue to cook for about 15 minutes, adding a little broth as necessary to keep the meat from sticking.

Spoon the cooked polenta onto one or two serving plates, top with the skewers and serve sprinkled with some parsley.

SPICY SAUSAGE & POLENTA LASAGNE

LASAGNE DI SALSICCIA PICCANTE E POLENTA

Hearty and delicious, this lasagne – which uses polenta in place of pasta sheets – is a real crowd pleaser.

1½ teaspoons olive oil

1 onion, finely chopped

1 celery stalk/rib, finely chopped

1 carrot, finely chopped

handful of freshly chopped
   flat-leaf parsley

6–8 Italian sausages, casings
   removed (see Note)

2 garlic cloves, finely sliced

1 teaspoon dried chilli/hot red
   pepper flakes

2 x 400-g/14-oz. cans plum
   tomatoes

1 quantity of basic polenta
   (see page 83)

100 g/3½ oz. pecorino, freshly
   grated

150 g/5½ oz. mozzarella,
   cut into thin slices

sea salt and freshly ground
   black pepper

crusty bread, to serve

Serves 4–6

Heat the oil in a saucepan over a low heat, add the onion, celery and carrot and cook slowly until lightly coloured.

Crumble the sausage meat into the pan, then break up any large clumps with a spoon. Add the garlic, chilli flakes and tomatoes and simmer for 40 minutes, adjusting the flavours as you go. At the end, add the chopped parsley.

Preheat the oven to 180°C/160°C fan/350°F/Gas 4.

Lightly oil an ovenproof dish (about 23 cm/9 inch square). Cover the base of the dish with one-third of the sausage and tomato sauce, then add a thin layer of polenta. Sprinkle over one-third of the grated pecorino and lay one-third of the mozzarella slices on top. Repeat these layers twice more, finishing with a layer of polenta and the two cheeses. Bake in the preheated oven for 40 minutes until bubbly and golden. Leave to stand for 5–10 minutes before serving with crusty bread.

Note: *Using good-quality sausages is a must – I love the fennel and red wine varieties for this dish.*

WHAT TO DRINK

Spicy foods call for a either bit of spice in the wine or some sweetness to act as a counterpoint to the spice. In the Veneto we get both in the king of the region, Amarone della Valpolicella! A lovely choice would be Il Lussurioso by Buglioni. A dry, smooth, yet powerful wine with intense flavours of red and black cherries and just a hint of white pepper. This sweet and spicy combination elevates a spicy dish to the next level.

BAKED POLENTA WITH SALAMI & TOMATOES

POLENTA PASTICCIATA

When polenta is baked as a pie, it is known as *polenta pasticciata*. There are many different versions – probably as many as there are homes in northern Italy – but this one is easy to make and is sure to draw compliments when served.

1 litre/4 cups water or vegetable stock
225 g/8 oz. coarse polenta/cornmeal
85 g/⅓ cup unsalted butter
300 g/10½ oz. mixed mushrooms (chestnut, field, porcini or cep), cleaned and sliced
1 x 400-g/14-oz. can Italian plum tomatoes, drained, seeds squeezed out and chopped
175 g/6 oz. Italian salami, thinly sliced
1 quantity Béchamel Sauce (see below)
55 g/2 oz. Parmesan, grated
sea salt and freshly ground black pepper

Serves 4

Place the water or stock in a large saucepan and bring to the boil. Gradually whisk in the polenta. Reduce the heat and simmer for about 20 minutes, stirring frequently. Season to taste.

Preheat the oven to 200°C/180°C fan/400°F/Gas 6.

Melt half of the butter in a frying pan/skillet and cook the mushrooms over a low heat for 2–3 minutes. Season to taste with black pepper.

Remove the polenta from the heat and stir through the remaining butter. Spread one-third of the polenta over the base of a greased ovenproof dish. Top with one-third of the mushrooms, one-third of the tomatoes, one-third of the salami and one-third of the béchamel sauce. Repeat these layers twice more, ending with a final layer of béchamel sauce, then sprinkle over the grated Parmesan. Bake in the preheated oven for 30 minutes until bubbly and golden. Leave to stand for 5–10 minutes before serving.

BÉCHAMEL SAUCE

BESCIAMELLA

Besciamella is best made with Italian '00' flour. The flour is so finely milled that it avoids the danger of lumps during mixing. It also has very low gluten levels and so makes a much lighter sauce.

20 g/1⅓ tablespoons unsalted butter
1 litre/4 cups milk or stock, warmed
40 g/¼ cup Italian '00' flour
1 teaspoon finely grated nutmeg

Makes about 1 litre/4 cups

Melt the butter in a saucepan. Mix in the flour, ensuring there are no lumps. Add the warm milk or broth and some salt, then slowly bring the mixture to the boil. Continue stirring until the sauce becomes thick and creamy. Taste to check the seasoning, adding more salt and nutmeg as needed.

FRIED POLENTA & FONTINA SANDWICHES

POLENTA FRITTA CON FONTINA

Serve with a crisp salad for a light lunch or as a *merenda* (a snack between lunch and dinner).

1 quantity of basic
   polenta (see page 83)
250 g/9 oz. Fontina or
   Gruyère cheese
100 g/2 cups wild
   rocket/arugula
50 g/1/3 cup Italian '00'
   flour
2 large/US extra-large
   eggs, lightly beaten

100 g/3½ oz. dried
   breadcrumbs
sea salt and freshly
   ground black pepper
olive oil, for frying

loaf tin/bread pan

Serves 4–6

Prepare the polenta following the instructions on page 83 (but do not bake it). Spoon the polenta into a loaf tin/bread pan and leave to set for several hours. It must be firm enough to cut into slices.

Turn the polenta loaf out of the tin and cut it into 1-cm/½-inch thick slices, about 9 cm/3½ inches big. Cover half the polenta slices with the cheese, rocket and some seasoning. Place the other slices of polenta on top to make sandwiches and press firmly together so the filling will not fall out.

Dip each sandwich first in the flour, then the beaten eggs, then lastly the breadcrumbs. I recommend leaving the sandwiches to chill in the fridge for 1½ hours before frying.

Heat a little olive oil in a frying pan/skillet and fry the polenta sandwiches in batches, a few at a time, on both sides until golden. Transfer the fried sandwiches to a plate lined with paper towels to drain. Keep warm while you cook the rest of the sandwiches, then serve hot.

POTATO GNOCCHI
GNOCCHI DI PATATE

The word *gnocco* literally translated means 'little lump', which is precisely what a *gnocco* is. There are so many ready-prepared poor imitations available to buy, so I urge you to spend some time making them yourself - the results are infinitely superior. I use old potatoes here, rather than waxy new ones, because the starch is fully developed and helps the gnocchi to stay together. I have served mine with a classic tomato and basil sauce.

SAUCE

450 g/1 lb. ripe tomatoes or a 400-g/14-oz. can Italian plum tomatoes

1 tablespoon olive oil

1 small onion, finely chopped

1 garlic clove, crushed

150 ml/²/₃ cup vegetable stock or water

1 tablespoon tomato purée/ paste

pinch of caster/granulated sugar

handful of fresh basil leaves, torn (optional)

1 tablespoon dry white wine

sea salt and freshly ground black pepper

GNOCCHI

900 g/2 lb. even-sized old potatoes (Maris Piper, King Edward, Desirée)

225-275g/8-10 oz. Italian '00' flour, plus extra for dusting

2 small eggs

50 g/3¹/₂ tablespoons softened unsalted butter, cubed

freshly grated Parmesan, to serve

Serves 4-6

First make the sauce. If using fresh tomatoes, put them in a bowl, cover with boiling water for 30 seconds, then plunge into cold water. Using a sharp knife, peel off the skins, cut the tomatoes in half, discard the seeds, then roughly chop the flesh.

Heat the oil in a saucepan, add the onion and cook gently for 5 minutes until softened. Add the tomatoes (fresh or canned) and garlic, cover and cook over a gentle heat for 10 minutes, stirring occasionally. Add the stock or water, tomato purée, sugar, basil (if using) and salt and pepper to taste. Half cover the pan and simmer for 20 minutes, stirring occasionally.

For a smooth sauce, pass the tomato mixture through a sieve/strainer into a clean pan and discard what remains in the sieve. Bring the sauce (smooth or chunky) to the boil, add the wine and keep the pan to one side, off the heat.

Meanwhile make the gnocchi. Cook the potatoes in their skins in a pan of boiling water for 20 minutes until tender (or longer, depending on size). Drain well and set aside to cool. Once the potatoes are cool enough to handle, peel off the skins.

Sift the flour into a bowl and make a well in the centre. Crack the eggs into the well. Push the cooked potatoes through a sieve on to the flour and eggs, from a height to lighten the potato with air as it falls. Add plenty of salt and the butter. Mix thoroughly, then knead until soft, adding more flour if needed.

With floured hands, roll the dough into 2.5-cm/1-inch thick ropes, then cut into pieces about 2 cm/³/₄ inch long. Press a finger into each piece to flatten, then draw your finger towards you to curl the sides.

Bring a large pan of salted water to the boil. Drop in about 20 gnocchi. Lower the heat and cook gently for 2-3 minutes, allowing the gnocchi to bob to the surface of the water and counting for 30 seconds. Remove with a slotted spoon and keep warm. Repeat with the remaining gnocchi.

Warm up the sauce. When all the gnocchi are cooked, add them to the pan and toss in the sauce. Serve the gnocchi sprinkled with Parmesan cheese.

PUMPKIN & WALNUT GNOCCHI
GNOCCHI DI ZUCCA E NOCI

I first encountered this splendid dish in the cooler months of October and November in the Veneto. It truly celebrates the beautiful pumpkins and squash that are proudly displayed in the Rialto Market. Be sure to cut the pumpkin with a very sharp knife.

2 kg/4½ lb. pumpkin or squash (make sure it is firm)

4 tablespoons olive oil

100 g/¾ cup walnuts, plus extra to garnish if preferred

2 large/US extra-large eggs

½ teaspoon freshly ground nutmeg

50 g/⅓ cup Italian '00' flour, plus extra for dusting

50 g/⅓ cup potato flour

1 teaspoon baking powder

100 g/1 stick unsalted butter

3 garlic cloves, finely sliced

generous handful of fresh sage leaves

200 g/7 oz. pecorino cheese, finely grated

sea salt and freshly ground black pepper

Serves 6

Preheat the oven to 180°C/160°C fan/350°F/Gas 4.

Cut the pumpkin or squash in half horizontally and remove the seeds. Place each half on a baking sheet, then drizzle with oil and salt. Bake in the preheated oven for about 1 hour until tender, depending on size. Set aside to cool.

Meanwhile, roast the walnuts for 10 minutes on a baking sheet in the oven, then finely chop.

Scoop the flesh from the pumpkin into a bowl. Squeeze the flesh through a clean tea towel to remove any excess liquid. This ensures that the pumpkin has a strong, more intense flavour.

Place the squeezed pumpkin flesh on a clean work surface and mix in the walnuts, eggs, nutmeg, both the flours and baking powder and some salt and pepper. Mix well until fully combined. Divide the dough into walnut-sized portions and roll into 5-cm/2-inch long pieces. Place them on a floured tray.

Bring a large saucepan of salted water to the boil. Drop in about 20 gnocchi. Lower the heat and cook gently for about 2–3 minutes, allowing the gnocchi to bob to the surface of the water and counting for 30 seconds. Remove with a slotted spoon and keep warm. Repeat with the remaining gnocchi.

Meanwhile, melt the butter in a frying pan/skillet. Add the garlic and cook gently until starting to soften. Add the sage leaves and cook until lightly golden, then remove the pan from the heat.

When all the gnocchi are cooked, spoon the butter and sage over the gnocchi. Serve the gnocchi sprinkled with pecorino cheese and a few more walnuts.

RICOTTA & GORGONZOLA GNOCCHI

GNOCCHI DI RICOTTA E GORGONZOLA

As I write this recipe, I know exactly what I want to eat for supper. It fills me with nostalgia and happy memories. I would often cook it for lunches at Books for Cooks in Notting Hill, London, which I was lucky enough to prepare weekly for the customers coming into the store. It was always well received and does happen to give the impression that you have been slaving away in the kitchen!

GNOCCHI
400 g/14 oz. ricotta cheese
    (home-made, if possible)
125 g/1½ cups finely grated
    Gran Padano cheese
3 large/US extra-large egg yolks
125 g/4½ oz. semolina
2 teaspoons freshly grated nutmeg
sea salt and freshly ground
    black pepper

SAUCE
50 g/3½ tablespoons unsalted
    butter
100 g/3½ oz. Gorgonzola cheese,
    cut into cubes
40 ml/3½ tablespoons double/
    heavy cream
2 handfuls of freshly chopped
    flat-leaf parsley

Serves 4

Make the gnocchi first. In a large bowl, combine the ricotta with the Gran Padano cheese, egg yolks, semolina and nutmeg and season with salt and pepper. Mix together until well combined.

Oil a clean work surface and roll the ricotta mixture into rounds about 1½ cm/¾ inch in diameter.

Bring a large pan of salted water to the boil. Drop in about 20 gnocchi. Lower the heat and cook gently for 2–3 minutes, allowing the gnocchi to bob to the surface of the water and counting for 30 seconds. Remove with a slotted spoon and keep warm. Repeat with the remaining gnocchi.

To make the sauce, gently heat the butter, Gorgonzola and cream in a saucepan. Stir in the parsley when the sauce is bubbling. Arrange the gnocchi in a serving dish and pour over the Gorgonzola sauce. Serve immediately while hot.

Note: *The gnocchi can be made in advance and stored in the fridge until ready to cook.*

FISH, MEAT & POULTRY

PESCE, CARNE E POLLAME

A FULL PLATE

When it comes to main-plate ingredients in the Veneto, the choices are again dictated by geography. In Venice, with its lagoon facing the Adriatic, seafood inevitably takes pride of place. The marshes north and south of the city (*La Serenissima*) nurture many game birds and other animals. On the good farmland of the *terraferma*, watered by the River Po, cattle, lambs, pigs and poultry are bred. The mountains and forests produce venison and wild boar.

The Adriatic supplies Venice and the Veneto with wonderful seafood. You can see this at any fish market in the region, but particularly at the Rialto in Venice. There, in huge, water-misted displays, are sardines, anchovies, sole, bass, monkfish, mackerel, tuna and swordfish, with the occasional chunk of shark (known as *vitello di mare*, 'sea veal'). Also on offer are tiny squid, cuttlefish, octopus, scallops, shrimps, spider crabs, razor clams and little round clams. Mussels are grown on ropes in the lagoon near Chioggia. Eels come from the rivers flowing into the Adriatic; they are also bred in the lagoon. Baked eel is popular on Christmas Eve.

A speciality of Venice is a particular crab native to the lagoon, which has been bred there for about 300 years. Males lose their shells twice a year and are whisked straight from hatchery to market before they have time to grow a new one. These soft-shelled crabs, known as *moleche*, or *moeche*, are 'drowned' in egg, floured and deep-fried.

Spider crabs are prized as well, but in 2023, large blue crabs – probably imported accidentally from America – have bred in huge numbers in the lagoon, becoming a danger to the local ecosystem, laying waste to oyster, mussel and clam beds. Money has been raised to get rid of the invaders, but many restaurants have opportunistically peppered their menus with new blue crab dishes!

Fish and shellfish are cooked simply in the Veneto. Small fish are dredged in flour and grilled or dipped in batter and deep-fried, *fritto misto*. Sardines are grilled or fried, but are also marinated in vinegar, for a Venetian delight, *sarde in saor*. Anchovies appear often in Venetian cooking, in sauces for pasta (bigoli, for instance), for duck, and in the *salsa verde* for *bollito misto*. Larger fish are stuffed, grilled or fried, or served raw, like my *carpaccio de pesce*.

But perhaps the most unusual fishy offering of Veneto is air-dried cod. Cod is not found in the Mediterranean, but it has been extraordinarily popular in Italy for centuries (as it is in Spain and Portugal), imported from Scandinavia. Air-dried fish

– known as *stoccafisso* (stockfish) elsewhere in Italy – goes by the name *baccalà* in the Veneto (which generally refers to salted dried cod). Venice itself has its *baccalà mantecato*, fish which is reconstituted by soaking, then beaten with enough olive oil to render it silky smooth. (In 2001, a brotherhood was formed to protect and promote the dish, the *Dogale Confraternita del Baccalà Mantecato*). Vicenza has its own version, *baccalà alla vicentina*, which, after reconstituting, is cooked in milk with garlic, parsley, Parmesan and anchovies, sometimes with a hint of cinnamon, and served with white polenta.

Meat and poultry are eaten in the Veneto. *Bollito misto* (mixed boiled meats) is served with a *salsa verde*, usually for large celebratory parties. Veal is popular, usually cooked as small escalopes, but slow-cooked shin is also found. Veal liver, cooked as *fegato alla veneziana* (in the Venetian style), is one of Venice's most famous dishes. Obviously many restaurants will offer beef steaks to their international customers, but the most renowned use of beef is, again, a Venetian dish: in the 1960s, the founder of Harry's Bar, named his dish of raw slices of beef topped with, variously, mayonnaise, shaved Parmesan, oil or rocket/arugula, after the Venetian painter, Carpaccio. Warming stews, sometimes of horsemeat, are also favoured in Verona.

Lamb is eaten infrequently, usually at Easter, when it is still milk-fed and is roasted whole. Pork is popular, served roasted or braised in milk, a wonderful Italian invention, but the most ubiquitous use is in the big, rough-textured salami typical of the region, *soppressa*. (Vicenza has the only DOP version.) Another small salami from Verona is the quite rare (and expensive) *stortina*. There are good hams too, those from Veneto qualifying for DOP (along with others such as Parma and San Daniele).

Veneto is famous for its farmed, organic capons and chickens, many of the latter rare protected species. Chicken livers make their appearance in many pasta, polenta and meat sauces. Some farmers breed geese, which are used to make cured meats, and an unusual Paduan preserve called *occa in onto* (goose in fat).

Birds from the salt marshes include wild geese, but also many types of duck, including mallard, widgeon and teal, as well as guinea fowl, pheasants, partridges and quail. Pigeons were once kept for winter meat in dovecotes, in Italy as in England, and still feature in a warming and unusual baked dish from Treviso, *sopa coada* (layers of pigeon, bread, cheese and pigeon stock). Wild birds are often spitted and cooked whole on the mainland, perhaps over a tray of polenta to absorb the juices.

And many of these birds – as well as rabbits and hare – would be served with *peverada*, a peppery sauce that varies from town to town. Venice, Vicenza and Verona have their versions, but that from Treviso is most famous, using chicken livers, *soppressa*, anchovies, oil, lemon juice and, as its name suggests, lots of black pepper.

CREAMY SALT COD MOUSSE

BACCALÀ MANTECATO

Cod was introduced to Venice in 1431, when a Venetian captain brought a consignment to the city after a long stay in Norway. Venetians fell instantly in love with the fresh cod and found many ways to cook it. However, arguably the most popular is *baccalà mantecato* - a creamy, soft mousse-like dish, made with salt cod and served with polenta. Many *osterie* in Venice offer this version of the ancient recipe. Ragno quality salt cod is the leanest and best quality available and should always be sought out.

675 g/1½ lb. dried salt cod (Ragno quality, if possible), soaked for 48 hours in frequent changes of fresh cold water

140 ml/generous ½ cup light extra virgin olive oil (not too overpowering)

60 ml/¼ cup whole/full-fat milk

1 garlic clove, grated

2 handfuls of freshly chopped flat-leaf parsley

sea salt and freshly ground black pepper

crostini or polenta (see page 83), to serve

Serves 4–6

Drain the salt cod and discard the soaking water. Place the salt cod in a large saucepan and cover with fresh water, then bring to the boil. Reduce the heat to medium and cook for about 30 minutes. Drain the cod, then remove the skin and debone.

Chop the cod into small pieces and place in a large saucepan over a low heat. Beat the fish energetically with a wooden spoon, while slowly adding the oil and milk until it becomes a creamy, soft mousse. Season to taste, then stir through the garlic and parsley. Chill until ready to serve.

Enjoy spooned on top of crostini or served with polenta.

Note: *The salt cod should be kept covered in the fridge while it is soaking. See page 113 for more information about salt cod.*

FRIED SARDINES MARINATED IN ONIONS

SARDE IN SAOR

Saor in Venetian dialect means 'flavour'. It is a method of preservation used by sailors during long voyages. This is a wonderful dish that I totally relish. Please make it with the freshest sardines, be patient and wait two days for their ultimate flavour to develop. I feel so lucky that I have been able to shop for gloriously fresh sardines with my students at the Rialto Market for my Stirred Travel weeks. With very few ingredients, this is an iconic dish that I hope you will love as much as I do.

1 kg/2¼ lb. fresh
    sardines
30 g/¼ cup Italian '00'
    flour
olive oil, for frying
4 large onions, very
    thinly sliced
200 ml/scant 1 cup
    white wine vinegar

1 teaspoon caster/
    granulated sugar
sea salt and freshly
    ground black pepper
lemon wedges, to serve
    (optional)

Serves 4–6

To clean the sardines, remove the scales and cut off and discard the heads. Make a cut down the length of each sardine, open them out flat and lift out the central bone. Discard the entrails and gently wash the inside of the fish as the flesh is very tender. Pat dry with paper towels. Dust the sardines with flour.

Heat about 2.5 cm/1 inch of oil in a frying pan/skillet over a medium heat. Add the sardines to the pan and fry until golden brown on both sides. Remove with a slotted spoon and drain on paper towels.

Using the same pan and oil, sauté the onions over a medium heat, stirring occasionally. Add the vinegar and sugar, then stir until well combined. Cook for 5 minutes or until the vinegar has evaporated, then remove from the heat.

Arrange a layer of sardines in a serving dish, then top with a layer of onions. Repeat these layers until all the ingredients are used up. Cover the dish and leave the sardines to marinate in the fridge for up to 2 days, if you can resist.

STEWED CUTTLEFISH WITH BITTER GREENS IN TOMATO SAUCE
TOTANI IN ZIMINO

This recipe is said to be of Arab origin. The words *in zimino* come from the Arab word 'samin', meaning 'precious' or 'expensive'. Through the centuries it has come to signify a method of cooking fish in butter or olive oil with a sauce of green vegetables.

The Rialto Market in Venice has a fine display of cuttlefish. I always ask for the freshest and best, which are most often the smallest.

500 g/18 oz. cuttlefish, or the smallest squid available
5 tablespoons olive oil
2 garlic cloves, finely chopped
½ onion, chopped
1 celery stalk/rib, finely minced
1 leek, washed and finely minced
150 ml/⅔ cup dry white wine
4-5 ripe plum tomatoes, quartered
750 g/1 lb. 10 oz. Swiss chard or spinach
1 teaspoon chopped fresh chilli/chili
handful of freshly chopped flat-leaf parsley
sea salt and freshly ground black pepper

Serves 4

Clean the cuttlefish by removing the black skin, eyes, mouth, ink sac, face and interior and then washing it thoroughly. Cut the tentacles into small pieces and the rest of the cuttlefish into 1-cm/½-inch wide strips.

Heat 4 tablespoons of the olive oil in a heavy-based frying pan/skillet over a medium heat. Add half of the garlic and sauté until lightly golden. Add the onion, celery and leek and cook for about 6-8 minutes until softened but not brown.

Add the cuttlefish to the pan, season with salt and pepper and sauté for 3 minutes. Add the white wine and cook over a medium-high heat until it evaporates. Add the tomatoes and continue to cook over a medium heat for 20 minutes. (If using squid, reduce this cooking time to about 5 minutes.)

Meanwhile, rinse the chard, then blanch it in a saucepan of boiling water for 1 minute. Drain and then coarsely chop the chard. Transfer to a separate frying pan, cover and steam over a high heat for 3-4 minutes, turning often.

Wipe out the pan, add the remaining olive oil and sauté the chard, remaining garlic and the chopped chilli over a medium heat for 5 minutes. Season.

Stir the chard into the pan with the cuttlefish and cook for a further 5 minutes. Sprinkle with chopped parsley to finish.

STUFFED SARDINES
SARDE RIPIENE

Sardines are stuffed in many different ways all around the Italian coastline.
The rosemary and garlic in this dish identify it as Venetian.

800 g/1¾ lb. fresh sardines,
  cleaned
5 tablespoons white breadcrumbs
  (slightly dry)
1 tablespoon freshly chopped
  rosemary needles, plus an extra
  sprig to serve
2 tablespoons freshly chopped
  flat-leaf parsley
2 garlic cloves, finely chopped
6 tablespoons olive oil
juice of 2 lemons
sea salt and freshly ground
  black pepper
good fresh bread, to serve

Serves 4

Preheat the oven to 200°C/180°C fan/400°F/Gas 6.

Remove the heads from the sardines. Make a slit down the underside of each fish, open them out flat and place them, flesh side down, on a board. Press down along the spine to flatten and loosen the backbone, then turn the fish over and remove the bone. Gently wash the inside of the fish as the flesh is very tender. Pat dry with paper towels.

For the stuffing, combine the breadcrumbs, rosemary, parsley, garlic and plenty of salt and pepper in a bowl. Pour in 4 tablespoons of the olive oil and mix thoroughly.

With the sardines skin-side down, divide the stuffing between them, spreading it along the central line of each fish. Fold the sides back together, so that the sardines resume their original shape.

Place the sardines, side by side, in a lightly oiled roasting pan in which they fit snugly in a single layer. Sprinkle with salt and pepper, drizzle with the remaining olive oil and the lemon juice, and lay the rosemary sprig on top (for extra flavour). Bake in the preheated oven for about 15 minutes until the fish are cooked and a little crispy on top. Serve warm with plenty of fresh bread.

STUFFED SOLE IN SAFFRON SAUCE

SOGLIOLA RIPIENA CON SALSA DI ZAFFERANO

This recipe's classical preparation is a little nod to it's Middle Eastern origins and the history of trading saffron and dried fruit with the Venetians.

3 Dover soles, filleted

2 tablespoons sultanas/golden raisins

125 g/4¹/₂ oz. tender young spinach leaves, stalks removed

2 tablespoons pine nuts

2 shallots, peeled and very finely chopped

600 ml/2¹/₂ cups fish broth (see page 45)

20 saffron threads

125 ml/¹/₂ cup dry white wine

40 g/1¹/₂ oz. unsalted butter, cut into small pieces

sea salt and freshly ground black pepper

kitchen twine or cocktail sticks/toothpicks

Serves 6

Rinse the sole fillets and pat dry with paper towels.

Put the sultanas into a bowl, add 3-4 tablespoons hot water and leave for 10 minutes to plump up. Drain and pat dry with paper towels.

Season the sole fillets with salt and pepper on both sides. Cover each fillet with some overlapping spinach leaves and place some sultanas, pine nuts and chopped shallot on top. Roll up the fillets and secure them with kitchen twine or cocktail sticks.

Bring the fish broth to the boil in a wide shallow pan. Turn the heat down to medium, then add the fish rolls and cover the pan. With the liquid barely simmering, gently poach the fish for 6 minutes.

Meanwhile, put the saffron threads into a small mortar and pound with the pestle until crushed. Add 1 or 2 spoonfuls of the hot fish broth to dissolve the ground saffron.

Using a slotted spoon, remove the fish rolls from the broth and place on a warmed plate; keep hot.

Pour off half of the broth. Add the saffron mixture and wine to the remaining broth in the pan and boil over a high heat until reduced by half. Stir in the pieces of butter, a few at a time. When all the butter has been incorporated, taste and adjust the seasoning.

Spoon the sauce around the stuffed sole rolls and serve immediately.

SALT COD WITH TOMATOES & BASIL

BACCALÁ AL POMODORO E BASILICO

Salt cod is a peasant food, born of the necessity to preserve gluts and to have food that would be edible in winter. I think it is quite a delicacy, though.

675 g/1½ lb. dried salt cod
(Ragno quality if possible),
soaked for 48 hours in frequent
changes of fresh cold water
olive oil, for frying
1 tablespoon plain/all-purpose
flour, for dredging
3 garlic cloves, finely chopped
700 g/1 lb. 9 oz. canned Italian
plum tomatoes
1 medium dried chilli/chili pepper
(*peperoncino*), crumbled
sea salt and freshly ground
black pepper
handful of fresh basil leaves,
to garnish

Serves 6

Pat dry the soaked salt cod with paper towels and roughly cut it into 6-cm/2½-inch pieces.

Heat 1 cm/½ inch olive oil in a large frying pan/skillet over a medium heat. Once the oil is hot, dredge the fish, one piece at a time, in the flour. Add several pieces of fish to the hot oil and fry until golden and crisp on each side. Remove the fish from the oil with a slotted spoon and drain on paper towels. Continue until all the fish is fried.

Preheat the oven to 200°C/180°C fan/400°F/Gas 6.

Heat 2 tablespoons of the olive oil in a large sauté pan. Add the garlic and cook until golden. Stir in the tomatoes, chilli and some salt and pepper. Simmer for 15 minutes, breaking up the tomatoes with the back of a wooden spoon. If the sauce becomes too thick, add a little water to loosen it.

Arrange the fried salt cod in a single layer in an ovenproof dish and spoon over the sauce. Bake in the preheated oven for 20 minutes. Garnish with basil leaves, then serve immediately.

Note: *Baccalà is dried salt cod. First the fish is gutted and cleaned, then it is dry salted (usually on board) and dried. It is particularly appreciated in Mediterranean countries. Salt cod has been a popular food in this region and elsewhere since early medieval times. It is tough looking, hard and stiff, but not as stiff as stockfish, which is air-cured, unsalted cod. Salt cod is rather expensive, and so, if possible, buy prime pieces from the middle, rather than from the tail and fin ends. The fish is creamy grey in colour with a fine dusting of sparkling salt. It needs to be soaked for 48 hours, with the water being changed frequently, until softened. In Italy, it is sold ready to cook. There are many regional recipes, a majority of which are from the Veneto.*

FISH CARPACCIO

CARPACCIO DI PESCE

Italians have a long tradition of eating raw fish straight from the net and appreciate their different textures and tastes and this dish is a perfect example of that.

4 fresh fish fillets (tuna, sea bass, sea
    bream), very thinly sliced (see Note)
1 fennel bulb, thinly sliced
handful of chopped mint leaves
2 tablespoons extra virgin olive oil
juice of 1 lemon
sea salt and freshly ground
    black pepper

Serves 4

Spread the fennel over a serving plate and drape the fish slices over the top. Scatter the chopped mint over the fish slices, then drizzle with olive oil and lemon juice.

Leave to sit for 30 minutes for the flavours to develop before serving.

Note: *When slicing the fish, use a very sharp knife. It can be helpful to ask your fishmonger to prepare the fish for you. If possible, use a mild extra virgin olive oil from Liguria or Lake Garda.*

CRAB WITH LEMON

GRANCEOLA AL LIMONE

Granceole are large, very tender spider crabs found only in Venice, where they are considered a delicacy. They are served simply with lemon so as not to overwhelm their subtleness. For ease, use any type of crab available.

6 cooked spider crabs
    (each weighing about 200 g/7 oz.)
    - ask your fishmonger to cook and
    prepare it for you
18 lettuce leaves
125 ml/½ cup extra virgin olive oil
juice of 1-2 lemons
handful of fresh flat-leaf parsley,
    finely chopped
sea salt and freshly ground
    black pepper

Serves 6

Make a circular cut beneath the upper shells of the main body and take out the flesh. Remove and discard the entrails and stomach, reserving the coral if there is any. Clean out the inside of each shell and wash well. If you are buying ready-prepared crabs, this will already have been done.

Place three lettuce leaves on each plate and top with the crab shells. Mix the crabmeat with the oil, lemon juice, parsley and a little salt and pepper. Return the flesh to the shells. Scatter the coral (if any) over each filled shell, and serve.

Illustrated on page 116.

Note: *Crab is much loved in Italy. Many of the best recipes come from around Venice, where the spider crab reigns supreme. This curious looking creature has five sets of legs with two miniscule claws that are arranged around the body like the legs of a spider. Its shell is covered in sharp bumps. Large crabs and other smaller crabs are also enjoyed, the latter in fish soups and stews. Crab flesh can be eaten 'dressed' as here, or in seafood salads or pasta sauces.*

SEA BASS CREPES

CRESPELLE DI BRANZINO

I will never forget this light and fresh dish that I enjoyed on a trip to Verona with my father.

CREPES

1 tablespoon olive oil

1 large/US extra-large egg

50 g/⅓ cup Italian '00' flour

150 g/⅔ cup whole/full-fate milk

sea salt, black pepper and nutmeg, to taste

FILLING

2 tablespoons olive oil, plus extra for frying

1 garlic clove, crushed

500 g/1 lb. 2 oz. sea bass fillets

250 ml/1 cup white wine

200 g/7 oz. fresh Datterini cherry tomatoes, halved

small bunch of fresh basil or fennel fronds

1 quantity of Béchamel Sauce (see page 83)

Serves 4–5

FOR THE CREPES

In a bowl, whisk together all the ingredients for the crêpes. Leave the batter to rest; the longer it is left, the better it will be.

Evenly coat the base of a nonstick pan with a little olive oil. Heat the oil over a medium heat, then pour a small ladleful of batter into the centre of the pan. Gently roll the pan until a thin layer of batter covers the surface. Cook until the underside is golden, then flip over and cook the other side. Stack the cooked crêpes on a warmed plate and set aside.

FOR THE FILLING

In a large pan, heat the oil. Add the garlic and sea bass fillets to the pan and cook over a medium heat for 2-3 minutes. Pour in the wine and allow it to reduce a little. Add the tomatoes and basil or fennel, then simmer for about 6-8 minutes until the fish is opaque. Season well then leave to cool. Using a handheld/immersion blender, purée the mixture to a coarse texture.

Preheat the oven to 200°C/180°C fan/400°F/Gas 6.

Spread a tablespoonful of the fish purée onto one of the crêpes. Loosely roll up the crêpe and place it in a buttered ovenproof dish. Repeat until all the crêpes are used up.

Pour the béchamel sauce over the crêpes and bake in the preheated oven for about 20 minutes until golden.

PORK COOKED IN MILK

MAIALE AL LATTE

On the last evenings in October, when the temperature in the Veneto drops, I love to serve this to my *studenti* after a week of cooking classes. It is most certainly the meat of the region and it is an exquisite and elegant all-in-one dish.

1 kg/2¼ lb. leg of pork
3 tablespoons white wine vinegar
400 ml /1²/₃ cups white wine
3 tablespoons olive oil
1 onion, chopped into small dice
1 celery stalk/rib, chopped into small dice
1 carrot, chopped into small dice
handful of fresh sage leaves
4 fresh rosemary sprigs
3 garlic cloves, crushed
600 ml/2½ cups whole/full-fat milk

Serves 4–6

One day ahead, place the pork in a deep non-reactive dish and pour over the vinegar and white wine. Place in the fridge and leave to marinate overnight.

The next day, preheat the oven to 150°C/130°C fan/300°F/ Gas 2.

Heat the oil in a casserole dish/Dutch oven with a lid. Add the pork to the dish and brown the meat all over, then add the vinegar and wine mixture to deglaze the pan. Transfer the pork and any liquid left in the casserole dish to a bowl and set aside until needed.

In the same casserole dish, gently sauté the onion, celery and carrot for 10 minutes until golden. Return the pork and liquid from the bowl to the casserole dish, then add the herbs, garlic and milk and cover with a lid.

Place the casserole dish in the preheated oven to slowly cook for 3 hours until the meat is tender.

Remove the casserole dish from the oven and set it over a medium heat. Remove the lid and leave the pork to cook further until the liquid has reduced by half.

Transfer the pork to a carving plate, then strain the liquid left in the casserole dish through a sieve/strainer to remove any milk solids. Serve in a jug/pitcher alongside slices of the pork.

WHAT TO DRINK

This typically regional dish pairs well with another classic regional wine, Soave. A choice selection would be Pieropan La Rocca Soave Classico DOC. Made from 100% Garganega and, unusually, having had time on lees (aging on top of spent yeast) and in barrel, this is a richer, more full-bodied wine. The fresh acidity and mineral notes are beautifully balanced by rich fruit, honey and peach flavours. It is an elegant and well-rounded wine which complements well the roast pork.

PORK TENDERLOIN BAKED IN PASTRY

FILETTO DI MAIALE E PROSCIUTTO IN CROSTA

This is a recipe for a special occasion, whether you are cooking at home or eating in a *trattoria*. It is the Italian version – a poor man's version, perhaps – of Beef Wellington, but it looks very stylish and is perfect for entertaining, as it can be prepared in advance and kept in the wings, ready to go. It would be great served as part of a wedding meal or other celebration. I often serve this pork dish to my students on our last evening together.

450 g/1 lb. pork tenderloin
1-3 teaspoons freshly chopped
 rosemary
10 slices of Parma ham
 (*prosciutto di Parma*)
1 large/US extra-large egg,
 beaten, to glaze
sea salt and freshly ground
 black pepper

PASTRY
200 g/1½ cups Italian '00' flour
100 g/½ cup unsalted butter, diced
about 2 tablespoons ice-cold
 water, to bind

Serves 6

First, make the pastry. Mix the flour and a pinch of salt together in a large bowl, then rub in the butter until it resembles breadcrumbs. Add enough ice-cold water to bind the 'breadcrumbs' into a soft dough. Wrap the dough in cling film/plastic wrap and refrigerate for 20 minutes.

Preheat the oven to 190°C/170°C fan/375°F/Gas 5.

Lightly season the pork tenderloin, being more generous with pepper than salt, and sprinkle with the chopped rosemary. Wrap the pork in the Parma ham, overlapping the slices as you go. Place the wrapped pork on a baking sheet.

Roll out the pastry to slightly larger than the overall dimensions of the pork. Drape the pastry over the pork on the baking sheet, wrapping it under the meat – it doesn't need to be completely sealed if it doesn't quite reach. Brush the pastry all over with the beaten egg and cut slits in the top of the pastry to allow steam to escape as it cooks.

Place the baking sheet in the preheated oven and bake the pork for 40 minutes until the pastry is golden. Leave the meat to relax for about 15 minutes before slicing and serving.

Note: *This dish is not served with a sauce, it should be enjoyed just as it is.*

VEAL CUTLETS STUFFED WITH MOZZARELLA

COTOLETTE DI VITELLO CON MOZZARELLA

Veal is the most widely available meat in the Veneto. It is light and more easily digestible. This particular dish is extremely simple to prepare and is particularly enjoyed in the autumn/fall when mushrooms are in abundance.

4 veal cutlets (each weighing about 200 g/7 oz.)
125 ml/½ cup olive oil
150 g/5½ oz. fresh porcini or wild mushrooms, cleaned and sliced
1 garlic clove, sliced
2 tablespoons freshly chopped flat-leaf parsley
2 x 115-g/4-oz. buffalo mozzarella, diced
2 tomatoes, skinned and diced
115 g/1½ cups Parmesan, grated
50 g/3½ tablespoons unsalted butter
a few sprigs of fresh rosemary
225 g/8 oz. mixed salad leaves
sea salt and freshly ground black pepper
fresh basil leaves, to garnish

Serves 4

Preheat the oven to 190°C/170°C fan/375°F/Gas 5.

Slice the veal cutlets in half lengthways and flatten each half slightly. Season with salt and pepper.

Heat half of the olive oil in a frying pan/skillet and sauté the mushrooms with the garlic and parsley for 4 minutes until the garlic is golden.

Divide the mozzarella between 4 of the veal cutlet halves, along with a few pieces of tomato, some grated Parmesan and half of the fried mushrooms (reserve the rest for the sauce). Place the other veal cutlet halves on top, sealing the edges by pressing down with the back of a knife with a blade.

Heat the remaining olive oil with most of the butter in an ovenproof frying pan. Add the rosemary to the pan with some salt and pepper, then sauté the stuffed veal cutlets until golden brown. Transfer the cutlets to a baking sheet or dish and bake in the preheated oven for 8-9 minutes.

Meanwhile, place the remaining fried mushrooms in the frying pan/skillet with the veal juices still in it. Add the remaining butter, simmer for a few minutes and season well.

Arrange a pile of salad leaves on 4 serving plates. Place a veal cutlet in the centre of each plate, then spoon over the mushrooms along with any juices from the pan and garnish with basil, if liked.

VEAL NOISETTES WITH MUSHROOMS & GARLIC

NOISETTE DI VITELLO CON FUNGHI PORCINI

This is a Venetian classic. When they are in season, during the shooting period from the end of September to early October, fresh porcini are used for this recipe in Venice. However, I use field mushrooms as they are easier to find, but still provide those earthy notes to the dish.

2 tablespoons olive oil

250 g/9 oz. field mushrooms, sliced

2 garlic cloves, finely chopped

handful of freshly chopped flat-leaf parsley

a little '00' Italian flour, for dusting

8 veal noisettes (each weighing about 55 g/2 oz.)

50 g/3½ tablespoons unsalted butter

4 tablespoons dry white wine

sea salt and freshly ground black pepper

fresh bread, to serve

Serves 4

Heat half of the olive oil in a large frying pan/skillet and cook the mushrooms, garlic and parsley over a medium heat for about 7 minutes until tender. Keep an eye on the garlic to ensure it does not burn. Set aside.

Lightly flour the veal noisettes. Heat the remaining oil with the butter in a large frying pan. Add the noisettes and cook for 5 minutes on each side. Season, remove from the pan and keep warm.

Pour the wine into the pan and let it reduce slightly, then add the cooked mushrooms.

Arrange the veal noisettes in a serving dish and pour over the mushrooms before serving with plenty of fresh bread.

CALF'S LIVER VENETIAN STYLE

FEGATO ALLA VENEZIANA

For this classic Venetian dish, strips of calf's liver are fried very, very quickly
in butter and served with sweet onions braised in wine.

75 g/3 oz. unsalted butter

400 g/14 oz. onions, thinly sliced

125 ml/½ cup dry white wine

800 g/1¾ lb. calf's liver, trimmed
and thinly sliced

sea salt and freshly ground
black pepper

3 tablespoons freshly chopped
flat-leaf parsley, to serve

Serves 6

Heat half of the butter in a lidded frying pan/skillet. Add the onions
and cook for 5 minutes until golden. Add the wine and some salt
and pepper, then cover and braise the onions over a low heat, stirring
occasionally, for about 25 minutes until very tender. Remove the
onions and keep warm.

When the onions are almost ready, melt the rest of the butter in
a separate pan. Add the liver and sauté over a high heat for about
4 minutes until just cooked through. Add salt to taste, then combine
with the braised onions. Serve immediately, scattered with parsley.

ROASTED TURKEY WITH POMEGRANATE

TACCHINO ARROSTO ALLA MELAGRANA

The bittersweet nature of pomegranate provides the perfect balance to succulent turkey meat. It also looks
rather spectacular on a serving platter. Serve with bitter green vegetables, such as rape, wild hops and broccoli.

100 g/½ cup unsalted butter

1 young turkey (weighing about
2.2 kg/5 lb.)

12 fresh sage leaves, plus extra
to serve

4-6 pomegranates

sea salt and freshly ground
black pepper

Serves 4-6

Preheat the oven to 200°C/180°C fan/400°F/Gas 6. Butter a roasting
pan with 1 tablespoon of the butter. Butter the cavity of the turkey with
3 tablespoons of the butter and add the sage leaves. Season well. Rub
the skin with the remaining butter and season well all over. Roast in
the preheated oven for 20 minutes, then turn the heat down to
180°C/160°C fan/350°F/Gas 4 and roast for a further 50 minutes.

Peel the pomegranates and extract the seeds and juice. Set aside
about 200 g/7 oz. of the seeds for serving. Blitz the rest of the seeds
in a food processor, then pass the mixture through a sieve/strainer to
remove the empty husks. Pour two-thirds of the juice over the turkey.
Cook for a further 40 minutes, or until a probe thermometer reads
180°C/350°F when inserted in the inner thigh.

Remove the turkey and place on a carving plate. Serve with the
reserved pomegranate seeds and some sage leaves. Strain the juices
from the roasting pan into a jug/pitcher and serve on the side if liked.

Illustrated on page 131.

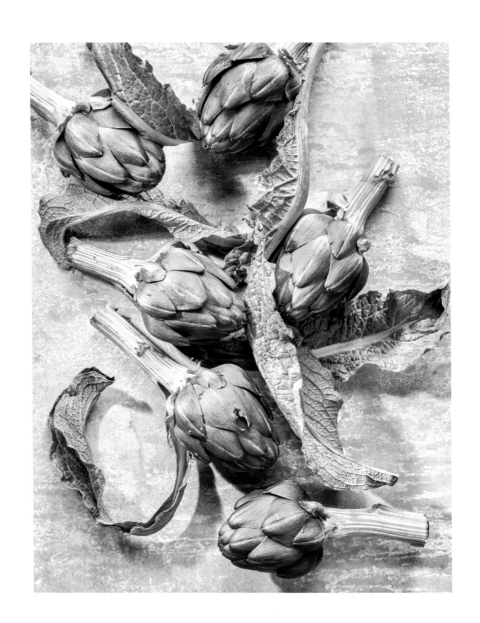

VEGETABLES

VERDURE

MORE THAN JUST A SIDE

As I have written before, vegetables are considered so important by the Italians that they have been given their own course within a formal Italian meal. This vegetable course is served after the appetizer, pasta and main plate, acting as a *digestivo*. Vegetables also have a major role to play in *antipasti*, the first course. Usually oily or vinegary, perhaps *sott'aceti* (pickled), *antipasti* vegetables stimulate the taste buds, so they have a dual role to play within the framework of a meal.

Italy has a considerable history so far as vegetables are concerned, and the country's approach to them has been influential throughout Europe for centuries. Italy was arguably the first European country to embrace the array of vegetables introduced from the New World, such as maize, tomatoes, potatoes and sweet (bell) peppers. Italy has also been the horticultural initiator of many new varieties of vegetable, being very much involved in the development of broccoli, fennel, celery and peas.

Vegetables are grown all over Italy, and the types vary enormously, according to geography. In the southern sun, vegetables such as tomatoes, aubergines/eggplants and courgettes/zucchini flourish, and characterize the local cuisine. In the less steamily hot north, including the Veneto, the produce is different. The rich alluvial plains of the Po Valley, with their hot summers and cold winters, are perfect for growing cereals such as wheat, maize, barley and buckwheat, as well as asparagus,

squash, artichokes, borlotti beans, hop shoots and, unique to Veneto, radicchio. In the hills and forests, there are also many varieties of wild mushroom, including, the prize of them all, the truffle.

Vegetables grown on the islands of the lagoon, or on the *terraferma*, are brought into Venice on *mototope* (boats). The name of these common Venetian working boats comes from the marriage of two separate words, *motore* (motor) and *topo* (rat or mouse: no, I don't know why!). Once rowed by hand, without a motor, these small vessels come into the city bringing with them the latest produce, from land or sea. Often the produce was actually sold from the boats themselves, and there are a couple of places in Venice still selling vegetables and fruit from the water. Occasionally the sellers of produce were women, and women have been associated with small Venetian boats, both in a working and sporting sense, for centuries. For instance, Venice boasts over 100 regattas a year.

Italians, more than any other nationality perhaps, enjoy and appreciate seasonality. Other countries were once the same, but now that vegetables and fruit are grown elsewhere in the world, then flown in throughout the year, growing seasons have largely lost their significance. Like my fellow Italians, I love the few weeks of the year when I can enjoy broad beans (wonderful with Pecorino cheese), or artichokes, or strawberries. Anticipating the arrival of specific produce to me is so exciting, and a rich part of the rhythm of the year.

Asparagus is grown on the *terraferma* and the islands, particularly on Sant'Erasmo. Just 30 minutes from Venice by boat, Sant'Erasmo is the largest - yet quietest - island in the lagoon. Its salty, rich soil is perfect for asparagus, especially the very thin young spears we know as sprue (*sparaselle* in Venetian). White asparagus - spears that have been cut underground before they reach the light of day - are grown in Bassano, in Vicenza. Asparagus is famously served with boiled eggs on the day of San Marco (25th April), the patron saint of Venice.

Sant'Erasmo is also famous for its purple artichokes. In the Rialto Market, I regularly see a man who sits all day, preparing *fondi* (artichoke hearts) for the market. Surrounded by discarded leaves,

he swiftly trims the artichokes until he has his beautiful *fondi*, which he stores in acidulated water. I buy these raw, then cook them for my students every September.

Pumpkins and other squash grow well on the *terraferma*, and they can be made into polenta, gnocchi and soup - but I like them best marinated. Beans of all kinds flourish in the Veneto, used fresh and dried in vegetable and pasta dishes, and soups. Courgettes/zucchini and fennel appear in the markets, as do *bruscandoli* (hop shoots), gathered in bundles to be used in risotto. The Italians are passionate about wild fungi, and the first foray of the year will be into the forests in March and May, in pursuit of the morel. Then from early summer, the hunt is on for ceps (the famous *funghi porcini*).

But the most famous vegetable associated with the Veneto is radicchio. My father exported it from Italy to the UK, and was the first trader to do so. Radicchio, a chicory, is bitter, and everyone thought Dad was mad as the British don't like bitter! But he persisted, and succeeded. There are three distinct types, two of which come from Treviso. The Castelfranco is round, mostly white, but speckled with red, as if someone had come along and splashed it with a paintbrush. The long variety most familiar in the UK is *radicchio de Treviso*. I serve this on my first night when I am teaching. I divide the plants into quarters lengthways, soak them in salted water to get rid of some of the bitterness, then drain and grill them until slightly charred. I season them and drizzle some pomegranate syrup on top. The third variety is the *radicchio di Chioggia*, a seaside town south of Venice. It is round and red and white, looking like a loose red cabbage.

MARINATED BUTTERNUT SQUASH CHIOGGIA STYLE

ZUCCA GIALLA DI CHIOGGIA MARINATA

Chioggia is a small town to the south of Venice that, today, has become famous for its high-quality produce such as beetroot/beets, radicchio, potatoes and pumpkin. This dish is traditionally made with pumpkin, but I have used butternut squash as it is more readily available all year round. However, I am eagerly eyeing my pumpkins growing at home, so feel free to swap them for the butternut squash as there are so many wonderful varieties available in the autumn/fall.

As an aside, something that I learned from the Venetians over the years is that you can use pumpkin blossom in the same way as courgette/zucchini flowers (*fritelle*) especially useful if you enjoy growing veggies.

2 butternut squash (weighing about 1.4 kg/3 lb. in total), peeled, halved, de seeded and cut into thin 1-cm/½-inch wide strips

45 ml/3 tablespoons olive oil

125 ml/½ cup red wine vinegar

1 large red onion, thinly sliced

1 large bunch of fresh basil

30 ml/2 tablespoons extra virgin olive oil (bold and fruity)

sea salt and freshly ground black pepper

Serves 4–6

Preheat the oven to 180°C/160°C fan/350°F/Gas 4.

Toss the butternut squash with the olive oil and a pinch each of salt and pepper, then transfer to an ovenproof dish. Bake in the preheated oven for 30 minutes

Meanwhile, place the vinegar, onion and some salt and pepper in a saucepan, bring to the boil, then remove the pan from the heat.

Arrange the squash in a glass roasting dish or serving dish, layered with some basil and a drizzle of the vinegar and onion mixture. Continue the layering until all the ingredients have been used up, then drizzle the surface with extra virgin olive oil. Cover and leave for at least 12 hours, or overnight.

Note: *This dish makes an excellent* contorni *(side dish). I always serve it with good bread to mop up the juices.*

PAN-FRIED MUSHROOM CUTLETS

COTOLETTE DI FUNGHI PORCINI

During the autumn/fall, when I'm guiding my students around the Rialto Market, we are always greeted with boxes of freshly picked porcini, heavy with their woodland scent. They are such a delicacy, so we devour them quickly. The farmers famously pick the mushrooms at first light; the wildlife equally adore them, so it is best to harvest them as early as possibly before any creatures take them. There are very many variations on this recipe, however I feel this one is most authentic and allows the earthy notes of the mushrooms to shine through.

100 g/¾ cup Italian '00' flour
2 large/US extra-large eggs, beaten
100 g/1¼ cups dried breadcrumbs
8 porcini, field or Portobello mushrooms, cleaned with a vegetable brush and thickly sliced
30 g/2 tablespoons unsalted butter
1 tablespoon olive oil
3 garlic cloves, crushed or grated
generous handful of fresh flat-leaf parsley, leaves picked
1 unwaxed lemon, cut into wedges, to serve
sea salt and freshly ground black pepper

Serves 4-6

Place the beaten flour, eggs and breadcrumbs in three separate shallow bowls. Dip the mushrooms in turn into the flour, then the eggs and lastly, in the breadcrumbs, ensuring they are evenly coated.

Heat the butter and oil in a frying pan/skillet over a medium heat, then add the garlic and fry until softened. Fry the breaded mushrooms in batches, a handful at a time, until golden brown. Remove with a slotted spoon and drain on paper towels.

Sprinkle the mushrooms with salt and pepper, garnish with parsley leaves and serve with lemon wedges on the side for squeezing over.

Note: *In the absence of porcini, field mushrooms or Portobello mushrooms offer an excellent substitute.*

ASPARAGUS WITH PARMESAN CHEESE

ASPARAGI ALLA PARMIGIANA

The Venetians have a love affair with asparagus that dates back to 200 BC. It has an eastern Mediterranean root. It grows so well along the riverbanks in the Veneto and so is on every menu during the spring time. The Rialto Market offers many different types of asparagus - wild, young, white, mature - and all are totally delicious. Any of the simplest cooking methods will do, in my humble opinion. Asparagus truly is celebrated in Venice more than anywhere else I know.

2 large/US extra-large
 eggs
150 ml/2/3 cup double/
 heavy cream
zest and juice of
 1 unwaxed lemon
60 g/2/3 cup grated
 Parmesan cheese,
 plus extra to serve

30 asparagus spears
handful of edible wild
 flowers, to serve
sea salt and freshly
 ground black pepper

Serves 4–6

Create a bain-marie. Bring a saucepan of water to a simmer, then set a heatproof bowl over the top of the pan.

Once hot, add the eggs and a pinch of salt and whisk until smooth. You must keep whisking, and keep the heat low to avoid the eggs scrambling. Add the cream, lemon zest and juice and whisk continuously until you have a thick sauce. Remove the bowl from the heat, add the Parmesan and seasoning, then set aside.

To cook the asparagus, snap the very bottom ends off at their natural breaking point by bending the spears and then peel the ends looks to make them look neat and tidy.

Plunge the spears into a saucepan of boiling salted water and cook until tender. This will depend very much on the size and age of the asparagus. Remove the asparagus.

Gently reheat the sauce if necessary. Serve the asparagus topped with the sauce and garnished with some extra Parmesan and a few wild flowers to finish. Enjoy.

Note: *Using a mix of green and white asparagus looks good together if you can get hold of the different varieties.*

SLOW-COOKED COURGETTES WITH MINT

ZUCCHINE IN PADELLA

I am quite fussy when it comes to this recipe as I love it so much. Always use small firm, freshly picked courgettes/zucchini that aren't overly large, otherwise the dish will end up too watery.

12 small, firm courgettes/zucchini (freshly picked, if possible)
30 g/2 tablespoons unsalted butter
1 tablespoon olive oil
3 garlic cloves, crushed
handful of fresh mint, leaves only, chopped
sea salt and freshly ground black pepper

Serves 4–6

Top and tail the courgettes, then cut them into thick rounds

Melt the butter and oil in a heavy-based saucepan over a medium heat. Add the courgettes and coat in the butter and oil, then add the garlic and salt. Turn the heat down to low and cook for about 40 minutes, partially covered, stirring occasionally, for the courgettes to develop in flavour.

Taste and adjust the seasoning, add the chopped mint and serve.

Note: *The courgettes must not brown as the flavour will be ruined.*

SPRING ARTICHOKES WITH YOUNG PEAS

CARCIOFI CON PISELLI

The Rialto Market sells the finest artichokes. Be sure to choose meticulously; they should be firm, heavy and squeak when you try to pull out a leaf.

8 baby artichokes, stems trimmed
2 unwaxed lemons
1 onion, finely chopped
2 tablespoons olive oil
250 g/1²/₃ cups freshly shelled peas
handful of fresh mint, finely chopped
handful of fresh flat-leaf parsley, finely chopped
sea salt and freshly ground black pepper

Serves 4

Remove and discard the artichokes tough outer leaves that have been exposed to the elements. Peel the stems and cut the artichokes into quarters. Immediately immerse the prepared artichokes in a bowl of water with the juice of one of the lemons.

Heat the olive oil in a large frying pan/skillet, add the onion and sauté over a low heat for 4 minutes. Drain the artichokes and add them to the pan. Season with salt and pepper and cook for 15 minutes.

Cut the remaining lemon in half, then slice one half into segments. Add the peas to the pan, cover and cook for 4 minutes. Drizzle with the juice of the remaining half lemon.

Transfer the vegetables to a serving dish and garnish with the lemon segments and chopped herbs.

Illustrated on page 146.

FRIED RADICCHIO FROM TREVISO

RADICCHIO ROSA DI TREVISO FRITTO

I find radicchio so incredibly versatile. I adore when I have the opportunity to change my students perception on it. I have had the greatest pleasure learning the glorious multitude of radicchio dishes from the Veneto at the hands of a local Nonna, and this is just one of the many examples dotted throughout the book.

4 heads of radicchio Treviso
100 g/¾ cup Italian '00' flour
2 large/US extra-large eggs, beaten
125-150 g/1¼-1⅓ cups dried breadcrumbs
olive oil, for frying
2 tablespoons shaved Parmesan
2 tablespoons pomegranate molasses
sea salt and freshly ground black pepper

Serves 4-6

Cut each radicchio into 4 pieces lengthways, then soak in cold water for 30 minutes.

Add a little salt and pepper to the flour in a shallow bowl. Place the eggs and breadcrumbs in two separate shallow bowls. Drain the radicchio and dry thoroughly, then coat in the seasoned flour, then in the beaten eggs and finally in the breadcrumbs, ensuring they are evenly coated.

Heat some olive oil in a large frying pan/skillet to a depth of about 3 cm/1 inch. Fry the radicchio quarters for 4-6 minutes, turning with tongs until crunchy and golden all over.

Arrange the fried radicchio on a serving plate, scatter over the shaved Parmesan and drizzle with pomegranate molasses.

BAKED FENNEL & CHEESE
FINOCCHIO AL FORMAGGIO

Making this dish recently for a group of students, everyone was a little alarmed at my method as everything seems to go into the oven very quickly and with very little fuss. The results were so good however, that I converted a few opinions.

Fontina is a truly celebrated cheese from high in the alpine meadows of Valle d'Aosta – the flavour for me is of honey, fruit and nuts. It is perfect with white truffles, if you ever have the opportunity.

6 fennel bulbs
50 g/3½ tablespoons
    unsalted butter
115 g/4 oz. Fontina
    cheese, freshly
    grated (blue cheese
    also works well)

freshly grated nutmeg
50 ml/scant ¼ cup
    whole/full-fat milk
sea salt and freshly
    ground black pepper

Serves 6

Preheat the oven to 220°C/200°C fan/ 425°F/Gas 7.

Trim the fennel bulbs, reserving any fronds for later, and discard the tough outer layers.

Cut the bulbs into small wedges and cook in a small amount of boiling salted water until tender. Drain and place in a greased baking dish.

Dot the fennel with a little of the butter, then season with salt and pepper. Cover the fennel with the grated Fontina, sprinkle with a pinch of nutmeg and pour over the milk.

Dot with the remaining butter, then bake in the preheated oven for 10 minutes until crisp and golden. Serve hot with the reserved fennel fronds scattered over the top.

Note: *Fennel bulbs are often referred to as either male or female. This relates to the two different natural shapes of the bulbs (male bulbs are elongated; female bulbs are round). There is no real difference in flavour once they are roasted, but like to use 3 male and 3 female when I make this dish.*

POTATOES WITH MUSHROOMS

PATATE CON FUNGHI PORCINI

Along the side of Italian roads in autumn/fall, you will encounter a host of vendors offering fresh porcini or ceps, all of them invitingly laid out in boxes and wrapped with fresh forest leaves. I always find it hard to resist, hence this recipe, which is a great way to enjoy these particular mushrooms. Watch out, as there can be little grubs in the stems: keep your eyes open and simply remove them – they won't do you any harm anyway!

500 g/1 lb. 2 oz. firm, waxy Italian potatoes (Elvira or Spunta are best)

400 g/14 oz. fresh porcini mushrooms or an assortment of wild mushrooms

5 tablespoons olive oil, plus extra for greasing

4-5 garlic cloves, crushed

handful of fresh flat-leaf parsley leaves, roughly chopped

sea salt and freshly ground black pepper

Serves 6

Preheat the oven to 180°C/160°C fan/350°F/Gas 4.

Scrub the potatoes and cut into 3-mm/1/8-inch thick slices. Brush the mushrooms to get rid of any dirt and cut into 3-mm/1/8-inch thick slices.

Lightly oil a large roasting pan and cover the base with a single layer of potatoes. Top with some of the mushrooms and sprinkle with the garlic, parsley, salt and pepper. Continue layering in this way until all the ingredients are used up. Drizzle over the olive oil, then pour 150 ml/2/3 cup water into the side of the pan.

Bake in the preheated oven for 1 hour or until the potatoes are tender and the mushrooms are golden brown. If the mixture seems dry, add a little more water. Serve hot.

FARMER'S SALAD

INSALATA DEL CONTADINO

Once, when I was walking in the fields surrounding the cookery school in the Veneto, I asked a couple of the workers what they had for lunch – it turned out to be this salad, which is rich in vitamin C. Broccoli is grown locally, although it is generally regarded as a southern Italian vegetable, appearing in the cooler months.

4 tablespoons extra virgin olive oil

3 tablespoons lemon juice

1/2 teaspoon dried chilli/hot red pepper flakes

500 g/1 lb. 2 oz. broccoli florets

250 g/9 oz. cooked or canned borlotti beans

handful of fresh flat-leaf parsley, finely chopped

sea salt and freshly ground black pepper

lemon wedges, to serve

Serves 4

First, make the dressing. In a serving dish large enough to hold the beans and broccoli, combine the extra virgin olive oil, lemon juice, chilli flakes, salt and pepper

Place the broccoli in a large saucepan of boiling salted water, add a glug of olive oil (this helps green vegetables to retain their colour) and cook until al dente. Drain and tumble the broccoli into the dish with the dressing.

Add the cooked beans and parsley and mix well. Serve at room temperature with lemon wedges for squeezing over.

Illustrated on page 6.

GRANDMOTHER'S BEAN SALAD

INSALATA DI FAGIOLI DELLA NONNA

As Italian bread goes stale so quickly, we have an infinite number of recipes to use it up, such as this one.

250 g/9 oz. cooked or canned
   cannellini beans
zest of 1 unwaxed lemon
6 tablespoons extra virgin olive oil
2 tablespoons red wine vinegar
1/2 teaspoon dried chilli/hot red
   pepper flakes
handful of mixed fresh herbs
   (parsley, thyme and oregano)
100 g/3 1/2 oz. country bread,
   cut into small cubes
sea salt and freshly ground
   black pepper

Serves 4

Drain the beans and leave them to cool.

Combine the remaining ingredients, except the bread and seasoning, in a large bowl and add the cooked beans.

Just before serving, mix in the bread and adjust the seasoning. Serve immediately.

Note: *Cannellini beans are low in fat and a source of slow-release energy, making this salad perfect for a lunchtime dish.*

RADICCHIO SALAD

INSALATA DI RADICCHIO

Colourful, flavourful and with the perfect balance of tastes and textures,
I make this radicchio salad for my students in Cison di Valmarino.

1 kg/2 1/4 lb. firm, waxy Italian potatoes
   (Spunta are best), unpeeled
45 ml/3 tablespoons extra virgin
   olive oil (bold and fruity)
2 tablespoons red wine vinegar
5 anchovy fillets in oil, finely chopped
1 plump garlic clove, finely grated
200 g/7 oz. cooked or canned
   chickpeas/garbanzo beans
1 fennel bulb, shaved on a mandolin
   (fronds reserved to garnish)
1 small radicchio, leaves torn
handful of fresh flat-leaf parsley,
   roughly chopped
sea salt and freshly ground
   black pepper

Serves 4–6

Place the potatoes in a saucepan of cold salted water. Bring to a simmer and cook until tender (the time this takes depends on their size). Drain the potatoes, allow them to cool, peel and then slice into 1-cm/1/2-inch thick pieces. Transfer to a serving bowl.

To make the dressing, whisk together the oil, vinegar and salt and pepper to taste in a small bowl. Add the anchovies and garlic and continue to mix together to create an emulsion.

Add the chickpeas, fennel and radicchio to the bowl with the potatoes, pour over the dressing and using your hands, gently mix to combine. Scatter over the fennel fronds and parsley. Serve with crusty bread to mop up the wonderful juices.

Illustrated on page 157.

DESSERTS

DOLCI

SWEETS FOR ALL TO ENJOY

Historically in Italy, desserts have not been of great importance. Nowadays, however, *pasticcerie* (pastry shops) entice us on almost every corner. They sell what could be desserts, but which are more likely to be eaten with coffee, possibly bought to be taken as a gift to a friend's house - for Italians never visit empty handed!

Desserts began appearing more prominently in Italian cooking in the 18th century. In the south, these would include almonds and dried or candied fruit, a nod to their Arabic heritage; in the north, they would be more bread or biscuit/cookie based. Nowadays, the occasional dessert will appear at a dinner or lunch party, served instead of fruit.

But it is fruit that still rules in the Veneto. Its rich farmland in the Po Valley, has an abundance of varieties: apples and pears in Verona, peaches in Treviso, cherries in Vicenza, as well as pomegranates, quince, melons, figs, loquats, medlars and grapes, of course, as the Veneto is a major wine-producing region (see Wines of the Veneto, pages 8-9. A *macedonia di frutta* (fruit salad) is popular during the summer, eaten both in restaurants and at home.

Italy is an important producer of kiwi fruit; they were first grown near Verona, and most plantations are now around Lake Garda. There are many nut orchards, too. An actual 'food forest', Bosco Nico, has been planted near Treviso; this reforestation plans to provide food, particularly honey, wild berries and nuts, at the same time as contributing to the ecology of the area and the planet.

Veneto produces many varieties of honey - once the only source of sweetness before the arrival of sugar. Producers in the province of Belluno, in the Dolomites National Park, are applying for DOP status for their acacia, chestnut, dandelion, rhododendron and wildflower honeys.

The Venetians were great traders and had the monopoly for many years on new products, such as sugar, spices and coffee. All sweet things contain sugar, many contain spices and some contain coffee, for Venice was the first city to popularize the new energizing drink and to open a house dedicated to it in 1720 (the wonderful Caffè Florian, which still exists).

The dessert most associated now with the Veneto is tiramisù, which famously uses coffee. Its origins are debated - it may hail from Friuli or Veneto, in the 1800s - but most think it was created in the 1960s by the owner of a restaurant in Treviso. There are many variations on the original recipe. If you visit Treviso in October, you might see competitors preparing their own individual recipes, both classical and creative, for the Tiramisù World Cup.

You will find other, possibly older desserts around Veneto: a bread pudding made with wine called *torta di pane ubriaca* (drunken bread pudding), a rice pudding and *risini*, small tartlets with a creamy rice filling, the latter from Verona. *Crema fritta* are small pieces of cold set custard, covered in breadcrumbs and deep-fried. Italy is famous for its ice cream, of course, and there are many renowned *gelaterie* throughout the Veneto.

Cakes are often baked for special occasions. *Fugassa* is a yeasted sweet bread from Venice, baked for Easter and Christmas. *Panettone* appears at Christmastime all over Italy, as does *pandoro*, which is a special treat for those from Venice and Verona. *Veneziana* is the Venetian equivalent of *panettone*: it is light, flavoured with spices and covered with white sugar crystals. (Actually these are all very similar.) *Pinza* is another cake, which in the Veneto is packed with dried fruit and nuts; it is baked at Epiphany (Twelfth Night), and eating a slice is said to bring good luck! And one of Bergamo's most famous dishes is a play on the Vicenza speciality, *polenta a osèi* (see recipe onpage 79): a sponge cake is covered with yellow marzipan (the 'polenta') and topped with little chocolate birds.

Venetians, whether in the countryside or cities, love their biscuits/cookies. They might eat a few for breakfast, perhaps with a coffee or glass of wine (during carnival time), or they bake them to store in a tin for guests, or to take when visiting. *Baicoli*, *bisse* and *zaleti* are specialities of Venice: the first are very crisp and light; the second are S-shaped and come from the Ghetto (Jewish Quarter) of Venice (usually made for Passover); and the third, meaning 'little yellow things' in dialect, are made with polenta. All are wonderful dipped into sweet wine or hot chocolate. Veneto *amaretti*, made with both sweet and bitter almonds, are glorious to look at.

Savoiardi (sponge fingers) are commonly used in *tiramisù*. *Bussolai* are buttery biscuits/cookies, made in 'S' or doughnut shapes, a speciality of the island Burano (where they are called *buranelli*). *Frittelle* are small fried balls of a doughnut-type mixture. *Galani* are sweet fritters made from long ribbons of dough shaped into a bow before frying.

Finally, a word on the Veneto's cheeses, many of which are DOP. Asiago, made in the town of Asiago in Vicenza, can be soft or hard, depending on age. Grana Padano is made in the Po Valley; very similar to Parmesan, it is not so crumbly. Montasio comes from the mountains (once made by monks), and is fruity and nutty in taste. Taleggio, a soft and creamy cheese, is produced in Treviso. Provolone valdepana is a stretched curd cheese from the Po Valley. All are cows' milk cheeses.

APPLE FRITTERS WITH GRAPPA

FRITELLE DI MELE CON GRAPPA

The Veneto region is well known for its apples. In some small villages, it is a fact that there are more apple trees than people. There is also a festival in the villages called *La Festa Della Mele*, where fruit growers are judged for the best varieties of apple. These apple fritters would be consumed by the village folk on this occasion.

2 large/US extra-large
　free-range eggs
100 g/½ cup golden
　caster/superfine
　sugar
300 g/2¼ cups Italian
　'00' flour
1 teaspoon vanilla
　extract
1 teaspoon ground
　sweet cinnamon
100 ml/scant ½ cup
　grappa or brandy

100 ml/scant ½ cup
　whole/full-fat milk
4 large apples
olive oil or groundnut
　oil, for deep-frying
icing/confectioners'
　or caster/superfine
　sugar, for dusting

Makes 20–25 fritters

Using a handheld whisk, beat together the eggs and sugar in a bowl until light and fluffy.

Add the flour, vanilla, cinnamon, grappa and milk, then continue whisking until the batter is smooth and foamy. Cover with a clean tea towel/dishcloth and leave to rest for 1 hour.

Pour enough oil into a heavy-based saucepan to reach about 8 cm/3 inches in depth, then gently heat to 180°C/350°F on a kitchen thermometer.

While the oil is heating, peel and core the apples and cut into 1-cm/½-inch thick slices.

Dip the apple slices in the batter, making sure they are evenly coated, then carefully lower them into the hot oil and deep-fry until golden. The thin slices should cook quickly, with no need to turn them. Remove with a slotted spoon and drain on paper towels. Dust the apple fritters with sugar and serve immediately while hot.

DEEP-FRIED CUSTARD BITES
CREMA FRITTA

This recipe goes far back in time. It was traditionally eaten between Christmas and Carnival time, but it can now be found at all times of the year. Serve while still hot with a Bellini (Prosecco with peach juice) or an Aperol Spritz.

5 large/US extra-large free-range egg yolks

80 g/⅓ cup golden caster/superfine sugar

200 g/1½ cups Italian '00' flour, plus extra for coating

2 teaspoons vanilla extract

1 litre/4 cups whole/full-fat milk

3 teaspoons ground sweet cinnamon

zest of 2 unwaxed lemons

2 whole large/US extra-large free-range eggs, beaten

100 g/2 cups fresh breadcrumbs

1 litre/4 cups groundnut oil, for deep-frying

icing/confectioners' or caster/superfine sugar, for dusting

20 x 20-cm/8 x 8-inch cake pan, lightly oiled

Serves 6-8

Using a handheld whisk, beat together the egg yolks, sugar, flour and vanilla in a heatproof bowl.

Bring the milk, cinnamon and lemon zest to the boil in a medium saucepan.

Slowly pour the hot milk onto the egg yolk mixture and stir to combine. Return the milk and egg yolk mixture to the saucepan and cook gently over a medium to low heat until the custard is thick enough to coat the back of a wooden spoon.

Pour the custard into the lightly oiled cake pan – it should be about 2 cm/1 inch deep. Leave to cool slightly, and then transfer to the fridge to cool completely for at least 3 hours. You can leave it uncovered.

Cut the chilled custard into 4-cm/1½-inch squares. Coat each piece first in a little flour, then in the beaten eggs, and lastly in the breadcrumbs. Chill in the fridge for 30 minutes.

Heat the oil in a deep frying pan/skillet to 180°C/350°F on a kitchen thermometer. Fry the coated custard squares until golden, turning once so they are golden all over. Remove with a slotted spoon and drain on paper towels.

Dust the custard bites with sugar and serve immediately.

Note: *Don't let any leftover egg whites go to waste - they can be frozen for another use or be used to make amaretti or meringues.*

ZALETI BISCUITS

ZALETI

These biscotti originated in Venice and take their name from the colour of maize flour.
In the Venetian dialect, *zaleti* means 'little yellows'. They appear in Carlo Goldoni's 1749 play
La Buona Moglie (The Good Wife) during an exchange between characters, where
they are mentioned as examples of inexpensive foods.

2 medium/US large free-range
egg yolks

80 g/¹⁄₃ cup golden caster/
superfine sugar

100 g/²⁄₃ cup fine polenta/
cornmeal

100 g/³⁄₄ cup Italian '00' flour

pinch of sea salt

2 teaspoons vanilla extract

100 g/¹⁄₂ cup/1 stick unsalted
butter, melted

grated zest of 1 unwaxed lemon

50 g/¹⁄₃ cup sultanas/golden
raisins, soaked in 2 tablespoons
rum

50 g/¹⁄₃ cup pine nuts

vanilla icing/confectioners' sugar,
(see Note), for dusting

Makes about 18

Using a handheld whisk, beat together the egg yolks and
sugar in a bowl until light and fluffy.

Add the polenta, flour, salt, vanilla, melted butter, lemon
zest and rum-soaked sultanas (drained) to the bowl with the
eggs. Add the pine nuts and mix well until fully combined,
then leave the dough to rest for about 20 minutes. This
allows the polenta to absorb the moisture.

Preheat the oven to 180°C/160°C fan/350°F/Gas 4. Line
2 baking sheets with baking parchment.

Divide the dough into 30-g/1-oz. portions and shape each
one into a thick, diamond-shaped biscuit/cookie. Arrange
on the baking sheets, spacing them apart.

Bake in the preheated oven for 15 minutes until golden.
As the biscuits cool they will become deliciously crunchy.

Once cool, dust well with vanilla icing sugar and enjoy with
a cup of coffee.

Note: *I keep a vanilla pod/bean in the storage jar with the sugar
to subtly flavour it with vanilla.*

CARNIVAL CRACKERS

GALANI

These delicate, sweet crackers are one of the emblematic sweets of the Venezia Carnival. My daughter Antonia and I, on a recent research trip, were offered these with coffee. They provided a tasty morsel with an excellent, interesting flavour; we enjoyed them so much that we had no room for dessert. In the absence of grappa, rum is a good substitute. Always serve these while warm.

250 g/1¾ cups Italian '00' flour, plus extra for dusting

3 large/US extra-large free-range egg yolks

1 teaspoon grappa or white rum

20 g/1½ tablespoons unsalted butter, melted

zest of 1 orange

1 teaspoon sea salt

2 teaspoons vanilla extract

50 g/¼ cup golden caster/superfine sugar

1 litre/4 cups groundnut oil, for deep-frying

icing/confectioners' or caster/superfine sugar, for dusting

Serves 6–8

Put the flour in a large bowl. Make a well in the flour, then add the egg yolks, grappa, melted butter, orange zest, salt, vanilla and caster sugar. Mix well until thoroughly combined , then leave the dough to rest for 1 hour at room temperature.

On a lightly floured surface, roll out the dough to a thickness of 5 mm/⅛ inch (as for a tart case). Dust the surface with extra flour, as necessary.

Cut the dough into 5-cm/2-inch squares. (I use a fluted wheel to create a frilly edge.)

Heat the oil in a heavy-based saucepan to 180°C/350°F on a kitchen thermometer. Working in batches, carefully lower 4 galani at a time into the hot oil and fry until golden. Remove with a slotted spoon and drain on kitchen paper.

Dust with sugar and enjoy warm or cold with a cup of coffee.

Note: *As with pasta and rice cooking times, the length of time it takes the galani to be fried until golden will depend on many things – the size of the pan, temperature of the oil, how many you fry at once. The important thing is to fry the galani until they are lovely and golden and crisp.*

VENETIAN BUTTER COOKIES

BUSSOLAI

Traditionally from Burano, these cookies can be recognized by their unmistakable shape, either a circular ring or an 'S' shape. The biscuits/cookies that I've bought at Marco Polo Airport in boxes have, in fact, been a ring shape, but I must say that the 'S' shape is far more attractive. Excellent with coffee or wine as a digestif.

3 large/US extra-large free-range egg yolks
100 g/½ cup caster/superfine sugar
250 g/1¾ cups Italian '00' flour
100 g/1 stick unsalted butter, softened
pinch of sea salt
zest of 1 large unwaxed lemon
zest of 1 large unwaxed orange
3 teaspoons vanilla extract

Makes about 18–20

Using an electric stand mixer or a handheld mixer, beat together the eggs and sugar in a bowl until pale and airy.

Add the rest of the ingredients to the bowl and mix well on a low speed until everything is fully incorporated. Leave the dough to rest for 1 hour in the fridge.

Preheat the oven 180°C/160°C fan/350°F/Gas 4. Line 2 baking sheets with parchment paper.

Divide the dough into 30-g/1-oz. portions and shape each one into an 11-cm/4-inch log. Form each log into an 'S' shape or a circular ring (both are authentic). Arrange on the baking sheets, spacing them apart.

Bake in the preheated oven for 18 minutes until pale on top and golden brown underneath. Share these cookies with friends, enjoyed as a *merenda* (mid-afternoon snack) or with coffee or wine.

FRUIT LOAF

ZELTEN

A recipe from the Dolomites, and one that is most certainly perfect around Christmastime as it is packed with warming spices. I have enjoyed many variations, but I like this one the best.

170 g/1¼ cups raisins

300 g/2 cups candied lemon peel, diced (buy whole pieces of peel and dice them yourself for the best flavour)

150 ml/⅔ cup grappa or rum

110 g/½ cup/1 stick unsalted butter

3 large/US extra-large free-range eggs

350 g/1¾ cups golden caster/ superfine sugar

700 g/5½ cups Italian '00' flour, plus extra for dusting

4 teaspoons active dry yeast

170 g/1¼ cups pine nuts

170 g/1¼ cups chopped almonds

170 g/1¼ cups dates, stoned/pitted and chopped

170 g/1¼ cups walnuts, chopped

2 teaspoons ground sweet cinnamon

1 teaspoon ground cloves

3 tablespoons whole/full-fat milk

icing/confectioners' sugar, for dusting

30 x 41-cm/12 x 16-inch baking dish

Makes 4 small loaves

Soak the raisins and candied peel in the grappa or rum for 1 hour.

Meanwhile, heat 75 ml/⅓ cup water in a saucepan, add the butter, then set aside and keep warm.

Using an electric stand mixer or a handheld mixer, beat together the eggs and sugar in a bowl until mousse-like. Stir in the flour and yeast, then pour in the melted butter and water and mix well.

Drain the raisins and candied peel and add to the dough with all the remaining ingredients. Mix everything together really well.

Butter and flour a 30 x 41-cm/12 x 16-inch baking dish, shaking off any excess flour.

Divide the dough into 4 equal portions, then shape each one into an oval loaf about 2.5 cm/1 inch high. Arrange the loaves in the dish, spacing them about 7.5 cm/3 inches apart. Prove for 1 hour, covered.

Preheat the oven to 180°C/160°C fan/350°F/Gas 4.

Bake the loaves in the preheated oven for 30 minutes until golden. Leave to cool on a wire rack, then dust with icing sugar. Cut into thin slices and serve.

ITALIAN RICE PUDDING
BUDINO ITALIANO

The Veneto and Venice are particularly associated with rice, as the crop is grown extensively in the Po valley. You can serve this pudding on its own, or with poached peaches (see below) or indeed any fruit.

225 g/8 oz. arborio rice
300 ml/1¼ cups whole/full-fat milk
300 ml/1¼ cups double/heavy cream
1 vanilla pod/bean, split in half lengthways
1 teaspoon vanilla extract
½ teaspoon sea salt
25 g/2 tablespoons unsalted butter
125 g/4½ oz. caster/superfine sugar

Serves 4

Put the rice in a heavy-based pan. Pour in the milk and cream with 6 tablespoons water, then add the vanilla pod and extract and salt. Bring to the boil over a medium heat, then turn it down until the milk is bubbling gently (just as you would for a risotto). Let it cook for 15–20 minutes; the rice will be soft when ready.

Remove the vanilla pod, then stir in the butter and sugar. Once the sugar has dissolved the pudding is ready. Serve hot.

Note: *Any leftovers can be left to cool, pulsed in a food processor and then frozen to make a truly wonderful gelato.*

POACHED PEACHES & RASPBERRIES WITH LAVENDER SHORTBREAD
PESCHE E LAMPONI IN CAMICIA CON PASTA FROLLA

One of life's greatest pleasures is enjoying cold poached peaches straight out of the fridge on a scorching day. This recipe is perfect for making when ripe peaches are in abundance.

SHORTBREAD
200 g/1½ cups Italian '00' flour
100 g/½ cup unsalted butter
50 g/¼ cup caster/superfine sugar
2 teaspoons fresh lavender, finely chopped, plus extra to decorate

PEACHES
450 ml/scant 2 cups rosé wine
120 g/½ cup plus 1 tablespoon caster/superfine sugar
3 strips of unwaxed orange zest
1 strip of unwaxed lemon zest
1 vanilla pod/bean, halved lengthways
6 peaches, halved and stoned/pitted
100 g/¾ cup raspberries

38 x 25-cm/15 x 10-inch baking pan

Serves 6

First, make the shortbread. Mix all the ingredients together by hand until the mixture looks like breadcrumbs. Line the baking pan with baking parchment and press the mixture into the pan. Chill in the fridge for 20 minutes. Preheat the oven to 170°C/150°C fan/325°F/Gas 3, then bake in the preheated oven for 20 minutes until golden. Sprinkle with more sugar and lavender. Cut into the shortbread triangles while still warm and place on a wire rack to cool.

Place the wine, sugar, orange and lemon zests, vanilla and 150 ml/⅔ cup water in a wide sauté pan. Bring to a simmer to dissolve the sugar. Add the peach halves and simmer for 15 minutes until soft. Transfer the peaches to a heatproof bowl and remove the zests. Bring the syrup up to the boil and reduce until thickened. This will take about 20 minutes.

Return the peaches to the syrup, add the raspberries and leave to cool and infuse. Serve with the shortbread.

Illustrated on page 179.

TIRAMISU

TIRAMISÙ

There cannot be a restaurant in the whole of Italy that does not serve a version of tiramisù, every version is claiming to be the best and the variations appear to be endless. I have tried for years to produce what I consider to be the ultimate tiramisù. It is what I originally enjoyed with my father in the Treviso area with family friends at a wedding celebration. As always, I was in pursuit of the original recipe, which eventually arrived in the form of a handwritten note. My ultimate recipe calls for several things: the finest coffee, chocolate and mascarpone should be used – no compromises! And please do make the savoiardi for the best results.

450 g/1 lb. mascarpone (see below)

3 large/US extra-large free-range eggs, separated

3 teaspoons vanilla extract

2 tablespoons icing/confectioners' sugar

200 ml/generous 1¾ cup whipping cream

2 tablespoons brandy

4 tablespoons dark rum

100 ml/scant ½ cup strong black coffee

20 savoiardi biscuits/cookies (preferably home-made, see below)

70 g/2½ oz. dark/bittersweet chocolate (70% cocoa solids)

MASCARPONE

2 litres/8½ cups double/heavy cream (at least 30% fat)

60 ml/¼ cup lemon juice, strained

SAVOIARDI

6 large/US extra-large free-range eggs, separated

2 teaspoons vanilla extract

150 g/1 cup Italian '00' flour

4 teaspoons baking powder

½ teaspoon sea salt

150 g/¾ cup caster/superfine sugar

28 x 23-cm/11 x 9-inch shallow dish

muslin/cheesecloth

Serves 8

First, make the mascarpone. Heat the cream in a pan to 180°C/350°F on a kitchen thermometer. Remove from the heat and stir in the lemon juice, then leave to cool. Once cool, pour into a sieve/strainer lined with a clean muslin, set over a bowl, and chill in the fridge for 24 hours.

Preheat oven to 180°C/160°C fan/350°F/Gas 4. Line a baking sheet with baking parchment and set aside.

To make the savoiardi, using a handheld whisk, beat the egg yolks in a bowl until thick, then add the vanilla extract. Sift in the flour and baking powder together.

In a separate, grease-free bowl, whisk the egg whites until stiff, then whisk in the salt and sugar until the egg whites are glossy and very stiff.

Using a metal spoon, fold the egg yolk mixture into the egg whites to form a thick batter. Drop tablespoons of the batter onto the baking sheet and form into fingers measuring 20 x 6 cm/8 x 2½ inches. Bake in the preheated oven for 10 minutes until golden. Transfer the sponge fingers to a wire rack and leave to cool.

Beat together the mascarpone and egg yolks in a large bowl until thick and creamy, then stir through the vanilla and icing sugar.

In a separate, grease-free bowl, whisk the egg whites until foamy and not too dry.

Beat the whipping cream until thickened, then fold in the mascarpone mixture, followed by the egg whites, until mousse-like.

Combine the brandy, rum and coffee in a shallow bowl. Dip each sponge finger into the coffee mixture and lay in the shallow dish to form a single layer. Spoon over some of the mascarpone and continue layering in this way, finishing with a final layer of mascarpone. Finely grate the chocolate over the top of the tiramisù and chill in the fridge for at least 2 hours. Always serve chilled.

Note: *Savoiardi are used in a wide range of other desserts, including Zuppa Inglese. Make up a batch and store in an airtight tin.*

FIG, AMARETTI & RICOTTA TART

CROSTATA DI FICHI, AMARETTI E RICOTTA

When the figs are ripe and succulent, this tart demands to be made. Full of classic Venetian tastes and textures, a small slice with an espresso is just enough to lift your day.

130 g/½ cup unsalted butter

250 g/9 oz. amaretti biscuits/ cookies

175 g/6 oz. full-fat soft cheese

500 g/1 lb. 2 oz. ricotta cheese

100 g/½ cup caster/superfine sugar

3 teaspoons vanilla extract

zest of 1 unwaxed lemon

2 tablespoons amaretto liqueur

12 ripe figs, trimmed and quartered

1 teaspoon crushed fennel seeds (optional)

23-cm/9-inch deep tart tin/pan with removable base, lightly greased

Serves 8–10

Preheat the oven to 170°C/150°C fan/325°F/Gas 3.

Melt the butter in a saucepan. Blitz the amaretti in a food processor, then add to the pan with the butter and mix well. Tip the mixture into the base of the tin, then press down with the back of the spoon to evenly distribute the crumbs. Bake the tart base in the preheated oven for about 10 minutes. Leave to cool.

Mix the soft cheese, ricotta, sugar, vanilla extract, lemon zest and amaretto liqueur together. Spoon the ricotta mixture evenly over the tart base. Chill in the fridge for at least 3 hours, then top with the quartered figs in a circular pattern. Scatter over the fennel seeds to finish, if using.

Note: *You may like to top the tart with a fig leaf syrup as I have done here. To make the syrup, combine 1 litre/quart water, 3 fig leaves and 150 g/¾ cup caster/superfine sugar, then boil together until thick and syrupy. Drizzle over the tart to finish.*

CHOCOLATE & HAZELNUT LAYER CAKE
TORTA GIANDUIA

This cake is rich and moreish. It is the ideal celebration cake.

160 g/scant 1¼ cups Italian '00' flour

30 g/2 tablespoons Dutch processed cocoa powder

2 teaspoons baking powder

½ teaspoon fine sea salt

150 g/5½ oz. blanched toasted hazelnuts, plus extra to decorate

175 g/¾ cup unsalted butter, plus extra for greasing

160 g/¾ cup golden caster/superfine sugar

4 large/US extra-large free-range eggs, beaten

3 tablespoons whole/full-fat milk

GIANDUIA CREAM

150 g/⅔ cup unsalted butter

150 g/1 cup icing/confectioners' sugar

175 g/6 oz. hazelnut chocolate spread

2 x 20-cm/8-inch round cake pans, greased and lined

Serves 12

Preheat the oven to 180°C/160°C fan/350°F/Gas 4.

Place the flour, cocoa powder, baking powder and salt in a bowl and mix well.

Blitz the toasted nuts in a food processor until coarsely ground.

Using an electric stand mixer or a handheld mixer, beat together the butter and sugar in a bowl until light and fluffy. Fold in the eggs one at a time using a rubber spatula, releasing any mixture that gravitates towards the top of the bowl. Add the ground nuts and flour, then combine well on a low speed.

Divide the batter evenly between the two cake pans. Bake in the preheated oven for 25 minutes until the sponges have risen and shrunk away from the sides of the pan. Leave to cool in the pans for 8 minutes, then turn out onto a wire rack to cool.

Once the cakes are cool, split each cake in half horizontally so that you have four sponge layers.

To make the gianduia cream, beat the butter until light and fluffy, then fold in the icing sugar and hazelnut chocolate spread.

Place a sponge layer on a serving plate and spread with one-quarter of the gianduia cream. Place a second sponge layer on top of the first and spread with more gianduia cream. Repeat for the remaining two layers. Scatter over the whole and halved hazelnuts to decorate.

WHAT TO DRINK

This cake pairs amazingly well with a sweet red wine made in a passito style or a Recioto della Valpolicella. For the passito style, the Accordini winery produce an Amandorlato 'il Forrnotto' which is unbelievable and highly recommended. The Poached Peaches & Raspberries (see page 177) would also pair well with this.

VENETIAN APPLE CAKE

TORTA DI MELE

This light Genoese sponge layered with apples is delicious with coffee for breakfast or for an afternoon snack. Try adding a little finely chopped rosemary to the cake mixture to elevate this delicious cake.

1-2 teaspoons vegetable oil

1-2 tablespoons dried breadcrumbs

125 g/4 oz. unsalted butter

500 g/1 lb. 2 oz. Golden Delicious apples

4 large/US extra-large free-range eggs

150 g/¾ cup caster/superfine sugar

150 g/generous 1 cup Italian '00' flour

1 teaspoon baking powder

pinch of salt

6 tablespoons whole/full-fat milk

finely grated zest of 2 unwaxed lemons, plus extra to decorate

icing/confectioners' sugar, sifted, for dusting

rosemary sprigs, to decorate (optional)

23-cm/9-inch deep cake pan

Serves 6-8

Preheat the oven to 180°C/160°C fan/350°F/Gas 4. Brush the inside of the cake pan with the oil, then coat with the breadcrumbs, shaking off the excess.

Melt the butter in a small saucepan and set aside to cool.

Peel, core and quarter the apples, then slice thinly.

Put the eggs and sugar into a heatproof bowl set over a pan of gently simmering water. Whisk for 10-15 minutes until the mixture is thick and pale, and leaves a trail when the beaters are lifted. Remove the bowl from the heat and continue whisking until the mixture is cool.

Sift the flour with the baking powder and salt. Fold half of this mixture gently into the whisked eggs and sugar. Slowly trickle the melted butter around the edge of the bowl and fold it in gently. Take care to avoid knocking out the air and losing volume. Fold in the remaining flour, then the milk and lemon zest, and finally the apple slices.

Pour the cake batter into the prepared cake pan. Bake in the preheated oven for 45 minutes or until a skewer inserted in the centre comes out clean. Leave to cool in the pan for 5 minutes, then turn out onto a wire rack to cool.

To serve, dust the top of the cake liberally with icing sugar and scatter over the lemon zest and rosemary needles, if liked.

PANDORO
PANDORO

This is the famous recipe from Verona and it is quite wonderful. There are many versions as the original recipe is a well-guarded secret, but this version is the closest I can get to it. Pandoro means golden star and the tin that is traditionally used is readily available to buy online.

40 g/2½ teaspoons fresh yeast
500 g/3¾ cups Italian '00' flour
3 large/US extra-large free-range
    egg yolks
200 g/1 cup caster/superfine sugar
200 g/1¾ sticks unsalted butter
1 tablespoon vanilla paste
2 large/US extra-large whole eggs
vanilla icing/confectioners' sugar
    (optional) (see Note, page 169)

20-cm/8-inch pandoro/star-shaped
    cake pan, dusted with icing/
    confectioners' sugar

Serves 8–12

In a large bowl, blend the yeast, 90 g/⅔ cup of the flour, one of the egg yolks and 10 g/2 teaspoons of the sugar into a soft dough. Cover with a clean tea towel/dishcloth and leave to rise in a warm place (about 20°C/68°F) for 3–4 hours.

Mix together 150 g/generous 1 cup of the flour, 2 tablespoons of the melted butter, 70 g/⅓ cup of the sugar, the remaining 2 egg yolks and the vanilla paste, then add them to the dough.

Knead the mixture thoroughly by hand until perfectly blended, then leave to rise again for a further 2 hours.

At this stage, incorporate the remaining flour, 50 g/¼ cup of the sugar, 30 g/2 tablespoons of the melted butter and the 2 whole eggs, kneading the dough energetically. Leave to rise for a further 2 hours.

When it is time to knock back the dough, roll it out flat and dot the surface with the remaining butter. Fold the edges of the dough into the centre to form a packet, then roll again and repeat twice. Leave to rest for 30 minutes, then roll out and fold for a final time.

Finally, form the dough into a ball and place in the pandoro pan. Leave to rise in a warm place (above 20°C/68°F) until the dough has risen to the edge of the mould.

Preheat the oven to 180°C/160°C fan/350°F/Gas 4.

Bake the pandoro in the preheated oven for 45 minutes, lowering the heat to 160°C/140°C fan/325°F/Gas 3 after the first 15 minutes. When golden, turn out onto a wire rack. Once cool, dust with vanilla icing sugar, if you can. If not, regular icing sugar will be delicious too.

Enjoy with an espresso!

INDEX

PICTURE CREDITS

ACKNOWLEDGEMENTS

For this page to be at the back of the book always feels so wrong; the wealth of talent behind the scenes needs to be celebrated at the front.

The biggest acknowledgment to Editorial Director, **Julia Charles**, for her tenacity and dedication and for giving me this opportunity again. I am thrilled.

Abi Waters with her wealth of knowledge and expertise and gentle guidance and good humour; shaping this book. The very many errors that you have spotted never making me feel dreadful, joyful to be working with you. Humble thanks and gratitude.

Susan Fleming, my very dear friend of extraordinary talent, we so enjoy our meetings and passionately discussing Italy; this might be our twentieth project and I feel so proud.

Claire Winfield, so peaceful, gentle and totally absorbed in her project. Her extraordinary eye for detail has enriched this book magnificently, *grazie mille*.

Toni Kay, I didn't know it was possible to improve on *Cucina di Amalfi* but I've been proven wrong, wow and double wow. Love your work for the rhythms throughout this book.

Kathy Kordalis, so wonderful to see you and work with you again, such dedication and beautiful cooking and styling - a true artist, full of passion.

Richard Lagani, for all your wonderful wine information and for adding an extra layer of detail that was so needed to embrace the wine of the Veneto. Richard is a wine expert and the proud owner and founder of Aperivino Belsize, a cosy little wine restaurant located on Belsize Terrace in North London.